Challenger SECOND EDITION 1

ADULT READING SERIES

Corea Murphy

New Readers Press

Images courtesy of:
p. 6, p. 10 p. 14, p. 18, p. 23, p. 27, p. 31, p. 35, p. 42, p. 52, p. 58, p. 59, p. 67, p. 73, p. 79, p. 80, p. 84, p. 94, p. 100, p. 101, p. 107, p. 108, p. 113, p. 114 © 2008 Jupiterimages Corporation; p.47 istockphoto.com

Challenger 1, 2nd Edition
ISBN 978-1-56420-568-1

Copyright © 2010 New Readers Press
New Readers Press
ProLiteracy's Publishing Division
1320 Jamesville Avenue, Syracuse, New York 13210
www.newreaderspress.com

Printed in the United States of America
9 8 7 6 5 4 3 2 1

Proceeds from the sale of New Readers Press materials support professional development, training, and technical assistance programs of ProLiteracy that benefit local literacy programs in the U.S. and around the globe.

Developmental Editor: Terrie Lipke
Contributing Writer: Nina Shope
Creative Director: Andrea Woodbury
Production Specialist: Maryellen Casey
Art and Design Supervisor: James P. Wallace
Cover Design: Carolyn Wallace

Table of Contents

The Long and Short Vowels

ā	ē	ī	ō	ū
a	be	I	go	rule
name	he	time	so	rude
save	me	ride	woke	tube
hate	see	nine	Jones	use
late	need	Mike	hope	fuse
	feel	fire		

ă	ĕ	ĭ	ŏ	ŭ
at	yes	is	Bob	but
am	let	if	job	mud
can	get	him	got	sun
had	ten	his	lot	up
has	bed	did	not	us
and	Eddie	with		

Words for Study

o'clock	would	said	of
was	friend	to	do
for	have	you	know
Mr.	the	money	park

Bob Is Late

Bob woke up at nine o'clock. He was late for his job. He hoped Mr. Jones would not fire him. Bob got a ride with a friend named Eddie. His friend Eddie did not have a job at the time.

Eddie said to Bob, "Is Mr. Jones going to fire you?"

"I hope not," said Bob. "I hate the job, but I need the money. If I had a lot of money, I would quit."

"If you do get fired, let me know," said Eddie. "Mike is going to the park with me at ten o'clock. You can go with us if you do get fired."

Mr. Jones did fire Bob, so Bob rode to the park with Eddie and Mike.

1 Read and Write.

1. The name of Bob's friend is Eddie.

_____

2. Do you know if he got the job?

_____

3. Bob and his friends had fun at the park.

_____

4. Mike did not know the rules, but Eddie did.

_____

5. Can you save money?

_____

6. He knows I am not late for the job.

_____

7. The sun woke Eddie up at ten o'clock.

_____

8. Bob did not feel he was rude to Mr. Jones.

_____

2 Read and Write. Note the silent e rule.

time Tim	**1.** _____ did not have _____ to go to the park.
tube tub	**2.** The _____ was for the _____.
not note	**3.** Bob did _____ get a _____ from Mr. Jones.
can cane	**4.** _____ you use a _____?
quit quite	**5.** Bob did not _____, but he was _____ late.

More Work with Long and Short Vowels

ā	ē	ī	ō	ū
date	we	mile	home	tune
gate	keep	bike	hole	duke
lane	meet	five	rose	huge
take	week	hire	joke	cute
ă	**ĕ**	**ĭ**	**ŏ**	**ŭ**
man	red	it	cop	cup
Dan	wet	sit	box	rub
dad	pen	six	mom	gum
bad	when	fix	Bob	hug
		which		

Words for Study

on	without	down	very
that	relaxed	okay	by
from	until	let's	or
how	want	around	work

Bob Meets Dan Rose

Bob had a date to see a man named Dan Rose. Mr. Rose had a home on Red Gate Lane. That was six miles from Bob's home. Dan Rose was a friend of Bob's dad, and he had a job for Bob.

The job was fixing bikes. Bob did not know how to fix bikes. But it was so bad to be without a job that he had said to his dad he would take the job.

Bob said to Eddie, "I hope I feel relaxed when I meet Dan. I do not have to see him until five o'clock."

Eddie did not want to let his friend down. So he said, "Okay, let's ride around until it is time to see him."

Bob was very relaxed by the time he got to Dan's home at five o'clock. Dan said he would hire Bob to fix bikes.

1 Read and Write.

1. Tim rode five miles on his bike.

_____

2. Eddie and Mike joked with the cop.

_____

3. The duke was quite rude to the man at the gate.

_____

4. Do you know if Mom is feeling okay?

_____

5. Dad said, "You can use the cup if you want to."

_____

6. Bob said that he would be home around six o'clock.

_____

7. The mud was so bad that Mr. Lane did not ride his bike to work.

_____

8. Do you use a pen to do the work?

_____

2 Read and Write. Note the silent e rule.

huge *or* hug   **1.** Mom needed a _____ box for the roses.

cute *or* cut   **2.** Mike had a bad _____ and had to go home.

meet *or* met   **3.** Eddie got to the park by six o'clock and _____ his friends.

use *or* us   **4.** It was so late that Mr. Jones wanted _____ to go home.

cope *or* cop   **5.** Tim knows that he can _____ with his job.

rode *or* rod   **6.** We _____ down to Dan's home to see how he was feeling.

hopes *or* holes   **7.** Bob _____ he can fix the bikes.

ate *or* at   **8.** "If you want to do the work, you have to keep _____ it," said Dan.

LESSON 3

More Work with Long and Short Vowels

bep

ā	ē	ī	ō	ū
Kate	beep	fine	rope	June
lake	jeep	mine	bone	nude
made	seem	wipe	Coke	mule
Dave	seen	nice	rode	cube

rod.

ă	ĕ	ĭ	ŏ	ŭ
mad	men	in	hot	fun
hat	set	sip	pot	fuss
nap	pet	lid	Tom	bus
jab	pep	kid	rob	bug

= long
ᴜ short

Words for Study

girlfriend	her	saw	sight
bank	as	horn	off
she	much	first	woman
loved	been	then	one

Eddie's Girlfriend

Eddie's girlfriend was named Kate. Kate worked in a bank. She was cute, and Eddie loved her. He would see her five or six times a week. Eddie hoped that Kate loved him as much as he loved her.

Eddie had met Kate at the lake. He had been with Mike and Dave in Dave's jeep. When Eddie saw Kate, he made Dave beep the horn so she would see him.

At first, Kate seemed mad at the beeping, but then she saw Eddie. It was love at first sight! Eddie and Kate had fun at the lake, and then she rode off with him in Dave's jeep.

1 Read and Write. Mark the vowels in these words.

1. fīré   5. woke   9. ate   13. jab

2. sĭp   6. sun   10. use   14. cute

3. cane   7. hole   11. me   15. keep

4. nice   8. bed   12. lid   16. rule

2 Read and Write.

<table>
<tr><td>

mad
made
mud

</td><td>

1. Dave got _____ when he saw the _____ on his jeep, and he _____ Mike wipe it off.

</td></tr>
<tr><td>

hat
hates
hot

</td><td>

2. When it is _____, the woman _____ to be without a _____.

</td></tr>
<tr><td>

sip
six
sit

</td><td>

3. At _____ o'clock, Bob and Eddie _____ by the lake at the park and _____ Cokes.

</td></tr>
<tr><td>

cope
cop
cup

</td><td>

4. The _____ did not know how to _____ with the bug he saw in his _____.

</td></tr>
<tr><td>

man
men
mine

</td><td>

5. The _____ did not know that five _____ worked in the _____.

</td></tr>
</table>

fuse used us	**6.** Not one of _____ knows which _____ is to be _____.
am as at	**7.** She is as mad _____ Tom _____ I _____.
Kate late dates	**8.** As a rule, Eddie is not _____ for his _____ with _____.
pen pet pep	**9.** Kate's _____ had so much _____ that she had to keep her in a _____ when she was working.

Changing the First Consonant Sound

ā	Dave	made	bake	came	ă	bad	cat	man	nap
	gave	fade	cake	game		fad	fat	pan	lap
	wave	wade	make	tame		sad	pat	tan	cap
ē	week	feel	meet	need	ĕ	bed	let	ten	yes
	peek	heel	beet	feed		fed	bet	den	mess
	seek	reel	feet	seed		led	net	hen	less
ī	quite	ride	bike	time	ĭ	sip	quit	six	win
	bite	side	hike	dime		rip	kit	fix	pin
	kite	wide	like	lime		zip	fit	mix	tin
ō	go	bone	hole	hope	ŏ	rod	pot	Bob	hop
	no	cone	mole	dope		cod	dot	mob	mop
	so	phone	pole	rope		nod	rot	sob	top
ū	tune	rule	use	cube	ŭ	gum	bug	tub	sun
	June	mule	fuse	tube		hum	dug	rub	run
	dune		refuse			bum	rug	cub	gun

Words for Study

lived	help	oven	behind
aunt	this	looked	put
Louise	last	also	went
didn't	out	herself	should

Kate Bakes a Cake

Kate lived with her aunt. Her aunt's name was Louise. Kate wanted to bake a cake for Eddie, but she didn't know how to bake. Aunt Louise said she would help Kate, but Kate refused her help. She would bake this cake without help!

At last, it was time to take the cake out of the oven. The cake looked like a joke. She ate a bite. It was bad! She fed the cake to the cat. The cat hated the cake also.

Kate was very sad. She was also mad at herself for refusing Aunt Louise's help. She dug a hole behind her home and put the cake in it. She hoped that Aunt Louise didn't see her.

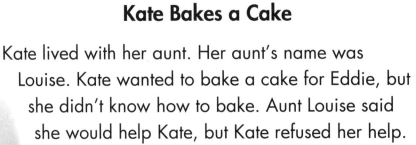

1 Read and Write.

cute or cut

1. The kid was so _____ that Aunt Louise gave him a hug.

tube or tub

2. Tom was in the _____, so he didn't get to the phone in time.

rode or rod

3. Bob used Eddie's _____ and reel at the lake.

Cap or Cape

4. Mr. Jones went to _____ Cod.

rip or ripe

5. The beet was _____, so Mike ate it.

ride or rid

6. Dan said to Bob, "Get _____ of that note. I do not need it."

win or wine

7. June likes to sip red _____ when she is relaxing.

fade or fad

8. Sitting on top of poles used to be a huge _____.

hop or hope

9. "I _____ you like fixing bikes," said Eddie to Bob.

fuse or fuss

10. When Aunt Louise saw how sad Kate looked, she said, "Do not make a _____. You should have seen the first cake I made."

led, less, *or* let **11.** Dave _____ Eddie use his jeep.

feed, feel, *or* feet **12.** Do you _____ like going to the park
with me?

hat, hot, *or* hit **13.** It was so _____ that Dave didn't go
bike riding.

him, hum, *or* ham **14.** Aunt Louise baked a _____ for Bob.

fade, feed, *or* fed **15.** Kate didn't _____ the cake to her pet.

2 Yes or No.

1. Do you have a bike? _____

2. Can you bake a cake? _____

3. Do you have a job? _____

4. Can you save money? _____

5. Do you like to joke? _____

6. Can you run a mile? _____

7. Have you been for a ride in a jeep? _____

8. Do you like to have lots of friends? _____

9. Do you make a mess when you bake? _____

10. Do you like getting help with this work? _____

Word Index: Lessons 1–4

A

a
also
am
and
around
as
at
ate
aunt

B

bad
bake
bank
be
bed
been
beep
beet
behind
bet
bike
bite
Bob
bone
box
bug
bum
bus
but
by

C

cake
came
can
cane
cap
cape
Cape Cod
cat
cod
Coke
cone
cop
cope
cub
cube

cup
cut
cute

D

dad
Dan
date
Dave
den
did
didn't
dime
do
dope
dot
down
dug
duke
dune

E

Eddie

F

fad
fade
fat
fed
feed
feel
feet
fine
fire
first
fit
five
fix
for
friend
from
fun
fuse
fuss

G

game
gate
gave

get
girlfriend
go
got
gum
gun

H

had
ham
has
hat
hate
have
he
heel
help
hen
her
herself
hike
him
hire
his
hit
hole
home
hop
hope
horn
hot
how
hug
huge
hum

I

I
if
in
is
it

J

jab
jeep
job
joke
Jones

June

K

Kate
keep
kid
kit
kite
know

L

lake
lane
lap
last
late
led
less
let
let's
lid
like
lime
live
look
lot(s)
Louise
love

M

mad
made
make
man
me
meet
men
mess
met
Mike
mile
mine
mix
mob
mole
mom
money
mop
Mr.

much
mud
mule

N

name
nap
need
net
nice
nine
no
nod
not
note
nude

O

o'clock
of
off
okay
on
one
or
out
oven

P

pan
park
pat
peek
pen
pep
pet
phone
pin
pole
pot
put

Q

quit
quite

R

red
reel

refuse
relax
rid
ride
rip
ripe
rob
rod
rode
rope
rose
rot
rub
rude
rug
rule
run

S

sad
said
save
saw
see
seed
seek
seem
seen
set
she
should
side
sight
sip
sit
six
so
sob
sun

T

take
tame
tan
ten
that
the
then
this
Tim

time
tin
to
Tom
top
tub
tube
tune

U

until
up
us
use

V

very

W

wade
want
was
wave
we
week
went
wet
when
which
wide
win
wine
wipe
with
without
woke
woman
word
work
would

X

Y

yes
you

Z

zip

Changing the End Consonant Sound

Long Vowels

ā	ē	ī	ō	ū
fade	beet	wine	note	mule
fame	beep	wife	nose	mute
face	beef	wire	nope	muse
cape	week	time	rode	tune
case	weed	tide	robe	tube
cage	weep	tire	role	
safe	seem	line	hole	fuse
same	seed	life	home	fume
sale	seep	like	hose	

Short Vowels

ă	ĕ	ĭ	ŏ	ŭ
tan	bed	hit	cod	hum
tap	bet	hip	cop	hug
tax	Ben	hid	cot	hut
jab	pep	mix	mom	bug
jam	pen	miss	mop	bun
jazz	pet	mitt	mob	bud
ran	wet	bit	pot	sum
rat	web	big	pop	sub
ram	wed	bid	pod	suds

Words for Study

talk	something	who	don't
after	problem	call	year
dinner	it's	Mrs.	about
ask	women	Ms.	only

Talking with Aunt Louise

Aunt Louise was Kate's aunt. She was also a woman Kate's friends liked to talk to. Bob went to see Aunt Louise after work. She was fixing beef for dinner.

"Can I ask you something, Aunt Louise?" asked Bob. "I have a problem at work, and I need help."

"But you said that you liked the job," said Aunt Louise.

"I do like it," Bob said. "It's not a big problem. The problem is that I don't know how to talk to the women who need bikes fixed. Should I call a woman Miss, Mrs., or Ms.? I bet talking to women is not a problem for you."

"Don't bet on it," said Aunt Louise. "Year after year, women and men get worked up about something. It is only a name. Would you like to have dinner with us?"

"Yes," said Bob, "I would love to."

It was fun to talk and joke with Aunt Louise.

1 Read and Write. Add -ed to these words.

1. look + ed = _looked_

2. last + ed = _____

3. talk + ed = _____

4. ask + ed = _____

5. mess + ed = _____

6. relax + ed = _____

1. face + ed = _faced_

2. save + ed = _____

3. joke + ed = _____

4. hire + ed = _____

5. line + ed = _____

6. refuse + ed = _____

1. hop + ed = _hopped_

2. sip + ed = _____

3. pat + ed = _____

4. gun + ed = _____

5. pop + ed = _____

6. sob + ed = _____

2 Read and Write.

bone, cone, *or* phone

1. If you want to talk, you can call a friend on the _____.

bug, bum, *or* bus

2. If you need a ride, you can take a _____.

safe, sale, *or* save

3. June wanted a robe, so she went to a _____.

bad, bed, *or* bud

4. A cot is a _____.

pan, pen, *or* pin

5. To bake a cake, you need a _____.

red, rid, *or* rod

6. Ben looked at the beet and saw it was

_____.

came, cane, *or* cage

7. If he cuts his heel, he can use a _____.

hit, hot, *or* hut

8. A duke would not want to live in a

_____.

bone, cone, *or* phone

9. After dinner, Dave gave his pet a _____.

bugs, hugs, *or* rugs

10. Aunt Louise loved Kate and gave her lots of

_____.

hope, horn, *or* hose

11. Mrs. Jones likes jazz very much, and she is saving her

money for a _____.

game, name, *or* tame

12. Dan didn't know Aunt Louise's last

_____.

pat, peek, *or* park

13. Mr. Jones refused to take his wife to the

_____.

lap, nap, *or* tap

14. When you sit down, you make a _____.

nd	and	end	bind	bond	fund
	band	lend	find	fond	funds
	hand	mend	kind	pond	refund
	land	send	mind		
	sand	spend	remind		
nt	ant	dent	hint	don't	bunt
	can't	rent	lint	won't	hunt
	pant	sent	mint		punt
	pants	went			runt
		spent			front
ck	back	deck	kick	hock	buck
	pack	neck	pick	lock	duck
	quack	peck	quick	rock	luck
	sack	check	sick	sock	lucky
	tack				
mp	damp		limp		bump
	lamp				dump
	ramp				jump

Words for Study

few	cards	casino	again	right
idea	online	won	maybe	himself
could	good	what	my	next
play	laptop	lost	are	happy

Eddie's Bad Luck

Eddie wanted to get Kate something nice, but he didn't have the money. He had spent his check on rent. He had only a few bucks to spend. Then Eddie had an idea. He could win lots of money!

Eddie was fond of card games. He loved to play cards online. His friends said betting on cards was a bad idea, but Eddie didn't see the problem. He had very good luck.

Eddie got his laptop and went to the online casino. He won the first game he played. He picked good cards from the pack. What luck!

Eddie won the next five hands. He was so lucky. He could get something for Kate and a lamp for his home.

Then Eddie lost a game. He played again and again. But his bad luck didn't end. He ran out of money.

Eddie was down in the dumps. "Maybe my friends are right," he said to himself. "Betting is a bad idea. Then again, maybe I can win big next time."

1 Read and Write. Add -ed to these words.

2 consonants

1. call + ed = _called_

2. hunt + ed = _____

3. land + ed = _____

4. walk + ed = _____

5. dump + ed = _____

6. end + ed = _____

long silent e

1. bake + ed = _baked_

2. name + ed = _____

3. like + ed = _____

4. date + ed = _____

5. tire + ed = _____

6. hope + ed = _____

short 1 consonant

1. rub + ed = _rubbed_

2. kid + ed = _____

3. rip + ed = _____

4. net + ed = _____

5. top + ed = _____

6. ram + ed = _____

2 Read and Write.

sack, sick, *or* sock

1. Bob was _____ of lending Eddie money. "I won't do it again," he said.

rent, spent, *or* went

2. Eddie _____ his check on the rent.

mind, find, *or* kind

3. Eddie checked his pants for money. But he didn't _____ one dime.

bucks, ducks, *or* luck

4. He had ten _____ to spend.

damp, lamp, *or* ramp

5. He needed to get a _____ for his home.

bond, fond, *or* pond

6. Eddie was _____ of card games. He loved to play cards and bet online.

buck, duck, *or* luck

7. He had very good _____ and liked to win.

band, hand, *or* sand

8. Eddie won the first _____ of cards and is very happy.

kicked, picked, *or* locked

9. He _____ good cards from the pack.

bind, find, *or* mind

10. Eddie didn't _____ that he lost the next game.

mend, end, *or* send

11. But his bad luck didn't _____, and he ran out of money.

More Work with Ending Consonant Blends

ang	ing	ong	ung
bang	king	gong	hung
fang	ring	long	lung
hang	sing	song	rung
rang	wing	wrong	sung
sang	thing		

ank	ink	onk	unk
bank	ink	honk	bunk
rank	pink		dunk
sank	sink		funk
tank	wink		junk
thank	think		sunk

Words for Study

clock	new	into	outside
day	car	left	dozed
downtown	all	there	once

The Wrong Side of the Bed

The clock rang, and Dave woke up in a funk. He wanted to sink back into the bed, but he had to get to the bank by nine o'clock. Dave had the day off from work. He needed to take money out of the bank so he could go downtown and look for a new car. He didn't want a new car, but he had junked his jeep. And Dave didn't like taking the bus to work.

He was all set to go when his cat, which was in the jam again, banged into a box of fuses that Dave had left out on the sink. The jam pot hit the sink with a bang. Bits of the pot cut Dave's face. There was also jam on his new pants.

"What a day this is going to be!" said a very mad Dave to the cat. "It's no use going out when you get up on the wrong side of the bed."

Dave wiped up the jam and kicked the cat outside. He went back to bed and dozed off at once.

1 Read and Write. Add *-ing* to these words.

1. go + ing = _going_　　　　　　**4.** look + ing = _____

2. fix + ing = _____　　**5.** miss + ing = _____

3. sing + ing = _____

1. take + ing = _taking_　　　　　**4.** joke + ing = _____

2. have + ing = _____　**5.** hope + ing = _____

3. live + ing = _____

1. run + ing = _running_　　　　　**4.** jab + ing = _____

2. sip + ing = _____　　**5.** hop + ing = _____

3. pat + ing = _____

2 Read and Write. Use the rule you know to read the new words.

| cat fat sat | **1.** Dave's _____ _____ _____ on the bed. |

| big pig | **2.** The cat is as _____ as a _____. |

| hole mole | **3.** A _____ was living in a _____ behind Bob's bed. |

ran fan ran	**4.** The cat _____ after the mole and _____ into a _____ .
date Kate late	**5.** _____ was _____ for her _____ with Eddie.
gave wave	**6.** She _____ Eddie a _____ when she saw him.
bank thank	**7.** Eddie said _____ you for the ride to the _____ .
remind kind wind	**8.** Kate said, "You were _____ to _____ me of the time. I didn't _____ my clock.
lamp camp	**9.** Mr. and Mrs. Jones went to get a _____ for the _____ .
pale sale	**10.** They saw a _____ pink lamp on _____ .
van man ran	**11.** Mr. Jones gave money to the _____ and _____ to put the lamp in the _____ .
fond find	**12.** Mrs. Jones was happy to _____ a lamp she was _____ of.

Review of Vowels and Consonants

fāce	sāle	cāge	lāke	jăb	păck	căt
race	pale	page	fake	cab	Jack	bat
lace	tale	wage	rake	dab	lack	fat
pace	male	rage	wake	lab	Mack	mat
ace	female	age	awake	tab	rack	sat

fēel	běnt	nīce	fīle	dĭg	kĭck
peel	went	rice	mile	pig	Dick
heel	tent	mice	pile	wig	nick
keel	lent	dice	tile	rig	tick
eel	cent	ice	while	fig	lick

phōne	jōke	lŏck		ūse	bŭg
zone	Coke	dock		fuse	jug
tone	poke	hock		refuse	lug
lone	woke	mock		amuse	mug
alone	awoke	rock		amusement	tug

Words for Study

never	were	just	fifty
an	where	here	stayed
they	over	done	now
your	some	ago	will

At the Amusement Park

Aunt Louise had never been to an amusement park. One day she talked her good friend Jack into going to one with her. As they rode in the cab, Jack said, "At your age, I can't see how you have never been to an amusement park."

"What do you think my age is?" Aunt Louise asked. She was getting mad. Jack didn't want her to make a fuss. So he talked about the fun they would have.

Once they were at the amusement park, Aunt Louise was happy again. She loved the rides and the games. She also liked the huge tents where she and Jack ate and ate until they just about keeled over. Then Jack said that they should go home while they had some money left.

"It seems as if we just got here!" said Aunt Louise.

"You should have done this years ago," said Jack. "The rides were only fifty cents then. We could have stayed a lot longer."

"In that case, let's stay now," said Aunt Louise. "Who knows how much money it will take to go to an amusement park next year."

"Okay," said Jack. It was no use talking Aunt Louise out of something once she had made up her mind.

1 Read and Write. Use the rules you know to read the new words.

| rode *or* code | **1.** Do you know your zip _____? |

| box *or* fox | **2.** The _____ hid in a hole until the man with a gun left. |

| ram, ham, *or* dam | **3.** At the meeting, the men and women said that the _____ needed to be fixed at once, or the town would have a big problem. |

| bad, pad, *or* add | **4.** Ben jotted down the note on a _____ by the phone. |

| five, live, *or* dive | **5.** Eddie liked to go to the lake and _____ off the dock. |

| fame, tame, *or* lame | **6.** Ms. Bond wanted to _____ a fox and keep it for a pet. |

| date, mate, *or* rate | **7.** At the _____ Kate was working, she would never make the meeting on time. |

| lined, dined, *or* pined | **8.** Mr. and Mrs. Jones _____ at six o'clock. |

2 Read and Write. Use *a* or *an* in these sentences.

1. Tim was very happy when he landed _____ eel in his net.

2. My cat had _____ dab of mud on her face.

3. Mack used _____ mat to wipe his feet.

4. Dan said to Eddie that he had _____ outside phone call.

5. Tom used _____ ice cube to get the gum off the rug.

6. The duck quacked again and again when _____ gun was fired.

7. Aunt Louise won _____ pink mug at the amusement park.

8. When Bob had _____ problem, he liked to talk with Aunt Louise.

9. Ben saw _____ ant on the deck.

10. Aunt Louise was at _____ age when she wanted to do all the things she had never done in her life.

3 Read and Write. Mark the vowels.

1. fūmé	5. tick	9. quick	13. us
2. lĕss	6. hand	10. cent	14. beef
3. neck	7. sock	11. mind	15. female
4. robe	8. safe	12. refuse	

4 Read and Write. Match the words that mean the same thing.

females	fun	✓huge	keep	six
fix	honk	jab	seek	weep

huge 1. big

_____ 2. save

_____ 3. look for

_____ 4. beep

_____ 5. five and one

_____ 6. poke

_____ 7. mend

_____ 8. amusement

_____ 9. sob

_____ 10. women

5 Read and Write. Answer these questions in good sentence form.
   New words: them quickly

1. When it is time to quit, do you relax or keep on working?

   _____

2. Do you like to go out on the town, or do you like to be at home?

   _____

3. Do you fix things that don't work, or do you get rid of them?

   _____

4. Do your friends think that you are happy or sad?

   _____

5. Do you take time on a job, or do you work very quickly?

   _____

6. Do you have lots of pep when you wake up, or do you feel tired?

   _____

7. Did you fix the last dinner you made in a pot or a pan?

   _____

8. Are you late for your dates, or do you get there on time?

   _____

9. Do you ask for help when you need it, or do you like to do all your work alone?

   _____

10. Do you like to phone your friends, or do you like to see them face to face?

   _____

Word Index: Lessons 1-8

A

a
about
ace
add
after
again
age
ago
all
alone
also
am
amuse
amusement
an
and
ant
are
around
as
ask
at
ate
aunt
awake
awoke

B

back
bad
bake
band
bang
bank
bat
be
bed
beef
been
beep
beet
behind
Ben
bent
bet
bid

big
bike
bind
bit
bite
Bob
bond
bone
box
buck
bud
bug
bum
bump
bun
bunk
bunt
bus
but
by

C

cab
cage
cake
call
came
camp
can
cane
can't
cap
cape
Cape Cod
car
card
case
casino
cat
cent
check
clock
cod
code
Coke
cone
cop

cope
cot
could
cub
cube
cup
cut
cute

D

dab
dad
dam
damp
Dan
date
Dave
day
deck
den
dent
dice
Dick
did
didn't
dig
dime
dine
dinner
dive
do
dock
done
don't
dope
dot
down
downtown
doze
duck
dug
duke
dump
dune
dunk

E

Eddie
eel
end

F

face
fad
fade
fake
fame
fan
fang
fat
fed
feed
feel
feet
female
few
fifty
fig
file
find
fine
fire
first
fit
five
fix
fond
for
fox
friend
from
front
fume
fun
fund(s)
funk
fuse
fuss

G

game
gate
gave

get
girlfriend
go
gong
good
got
gum
gun

H

had
ham
hand
hang
happy
has
hat
hate
have
he
heel
help
hen
her
here
herself
hid
hike
him
himself
hint
hip
hire
his
hit
hock
hole
home
honk
hop
hope
horn
hose
hot
how
hug
huge

hum
hung
hunt
hut

I

I
ice
idea
if
in
ink
into
is
it
it's

J

jab
Jack
jam
jazz
jeep
job
joke
Jones
jot
jug
jump
June
junk
just

K

Kate
keel
keep
kick
kid
kind
king
kit
kite
know

L

lab
lace
lack
lake
lame
lamp
land
lane
lap
laptop
last
late
led
left
lend
lent
less
let
let's
lick
lid
life
like
lime
limp
line
lint
live
lock
lone
long
look
lost
lot(s)
Louise
love
luck
lucky
lug
lung

M

Mack
mad
made
make

male
man
mat
mate
maybe
me
meet
meeting
men
mend
mess
met
mice
Mike
mile
mind
mine
mint
miss
mitt
mix
mob
mock
mole
mom
money
mop
Mr.
Mrs.
Ms.
much
mud
mug
mule
muse
mute
my

N

name
nap
neck
need
net
never
new

next
nice
nick
nine
no
nod
nope
nose
not
note
now
nude

O

o'clock
of
off
okay
on
once
one
online
only
or
out
outside
oven
over

P

pace
pack
pad
page
pale
pan
pant
pants
park
pat
peck
peek
peel
pen
pep

pet
phone
pick
pig
pile
pin
pine
pink
play
pod
poke
pole
pond
pop
pot
problem
punt
put

Q

quack
quick
quickly
quit
quite

R

race
rack
rage
rake
ram
ramp
ran
rang
rank
rat
rate
red
reel
refund
refuse
relax
remind
rent

rice
rid
ride
rig
right
ring
rip
ripe
rob
robe
rock
rod
rode
role
rope
rose
rot
rub
rude
rug
rule
run
rung
runt

S

sack
sad
safe
said
sale
same
sand
sang
sank
sat
save
saw
see
seed
seek
seem
seen
seep
send
sent

set
she
should
sick
side
sight
sing
sink
sip
sit
six
so
sob
sock
some
something
song
spend
spent
stay
sub
suds
sum
sun
sung
sunk

T

tab
tack
take
tale
talk
tame
tan
tank
tap
tax
ten
tent
thank
that
the
them
then
there

they
thing
think
this
tick
tide
tile
Tim
time
tin
tire
to
Tom
tone
top
town
tub
tube
tug
tune

U

until
up
us
use

V

van
very

W

wade
wage
wake
walk
want
was
wave
we
web
wed
weed
week
weep

went
were
wet
what
when
where
which
while
who
wide
wife
wig
will
win
wind
wine
wing
wink
wipe
wire
with
without
woke
woman
women
won
won't
word
work
would
wrong

X

Y

year
yes
you
your

Z

zip
zone

Vowel Sounds for y

y:	my	myself	cry	try	sky	why	
ay:	away	day	may	pay	payment	say	way
ey:	key	monkey	donkey				
oy:	boy	joy	toy	Roy	royal	loyal	
uy:	buy	guy					

day	**Days of the week**
today	Sunday
yesterday	Monday
birthday	Tuesday
payday	Wednesday
	Thursday
	Friday
	Saturday

wasn't	party	yet	little
none	please	since	what's
any	hurt	Min-hee	funny

A Birthday Party for Bob

Wednesday was Bob's birthday. His friends wanted to buy him something nice. Payday wasn't until Friday, and none of Bob's friends had any money.

Kate said she would bake the cake for the party, but Eddie said, "No, please don't. Let your aunt bake the cake. She said that she would. Why don't you pick up some wine on your way home from the bank?"

Kate was so hurt that she wanted to cry. She said, "Okay, but next time, I want to bake the cake."

Bob's friends didn't know what to buy for him yet. They only had a few bucks to get something nice. Dave said, "Since we don't have much money, why don't we play a joke on Bob and buy him some toys?"

Min-hee got mad at Dave. "Bob is not a little boy, you know. He is going to be 24 on Wednesday. What's he going to do with a lot of toys?"

Dave said, "Bob will think it's funny. Let's do it." So they all got into Mike's car and went downtown to buy Bob some toys for his birthday.

All the way downtown, Min-hee said to herself, "I think I am out of my mind to be going out to buy toys for a man's birthday."

1 Read and Write.

1. mess + y = <u>messy</u>

2. fuss + y = _____

3. bump + y = _____

4. need + y = _____

5. sand + y = _____

1. ice + y = <u>icy</u>

2. nose + y = _____

3. dirt + y = _____

4. bone + y = _____

5. wire + y = _____

1. fun + y = <u>funny</u>

2. sun + y = _____

3. Dan + y = _____

4. mug + y = _____

5. nut + y = _____

2 Read and Write. Note that the words below end in *-ly*.
Use these words in the five sentences.

| friendly | lovely | quickly | safely | weekly |

1. Mr. Jones did his work _____ on Tuesday so he would have time to buy his wife a new robe for her birthday.

2. Yesterday, Mrs. Jones looked up at the sky and said, "What a _____ day this is!"

3. "Don't fuss so much," said Aunt Louise to Kate. "I can get home _____ by myself."

4. Kate was happy working at the bank. The men and women who worked there were so _____ to her.

5. Bob had lent quite a lot of money to Dave for his new car. Dave said he would pay him back in _____ payments.

3 Read and Write. More words that end in -y.

Note: The *y* is changed to *i* in these words.

cry	cries	cried
try	tries	tried

Read these words in the sentences below.

baby (bā-by)

1. The _____*baby*_____ cries when his mom tries to put him down.

candy (căn-dy)

2. Dave gave Min-hee a huge box of _____.

sixty (sĭx-ty)

3. Bob's dad was _____ when he quit his job.

lobby (lŏb-by)

4. Eddie met Kate in the _____ at five o'clock.

ninety (nīne-ty)

5. There were _____ women at the meeting yesterday.

Andy (Ăn-dy)

6. _____ tried to buy Bob a kite for his birthday, but there were none left.

muddy (mŭd-dy)

7. The baby cried when he landed in the _____ hole.

handy (hănd-y)

8. Roy was so _____ that he fixed the sink in no time.

forty (for-ty)

9. When Jack takes a nap, he calls it "getting _____ winks."

Becky (Bĕck-y)

10. King Roy sat down to the royal dinner next to his loyal friend, _____.

4 Read and Write. Match the words that mean the same thing.

behind	hide	mock	Saturday
funds	joke	not happy	Sunday
funny	male	refuse	ten cents

_____ **1.** to keep out of sight

_____ **2.** in back of

_____ **3.** a dime

_____ **4.** man

_____ **5.** sad

_____ **6.** to make fun of

_____ **7.** to kid around

_____ **8.** to say no

_____ **9.** amusing

_____ **10.** money

_____ **11.** the first day of the week

_____ **12.** the last day of the week

Silent Letters

kn	wr	mb	ight	tch	tch
know	wrong	lamb	sight	catch	itch
known	wrap	climb	fight	match	ditch
knew	wreck	bomb	light	batch	witch
knee	write	dumb	might	patch	
knife	wrote	numb	night	watch	Dutch
knot	wrist	thumb	right	fetch	
knock			tight	ketchup	

Words for Study

movie	turned	stomach	I'll
minutes	green	told	waited
streets	gas	thought	worry
cell phone	too	breath	comes

Eddie Wrecks His Car

Eddie and Kate had made a date for Friday night. Kate asked Eddie to meet her downtown at six o'clock so they could watch a movie.

But on Friday, something went wrong at work. Eddie had to stay late. When he looked at his watch, it was five minutes to six! He jumped in his car and raced downtown.

Eddie saw a lot of red lights on the downtown streets. He knew he could call Kate on his cell phone, but he didn't want to get into a fight. He was late a lot, and Kate hated it. Eddie knew she would get mad.

When the light turned green, Eddie hit the gas. He didn't see the patch of ice until it was too late. His car landed in a ditch and wrapped around a pole.

Eddie climbed out of the car. He was numb. His stomach was in a knot. He knew the car was wrecked. How dumb of him!

Eddie got his cell phone and called Kate. She picked up right away. "Eddie, what's wrong?" she asked. "Where are you?"

Eddie told Kate about the wreck. He thought she might hang up on him. But she wasn't mad at all. She asked if he was hurt.

"I think I banged up my knee and wrist," he said, trying to catch his breath. "All I wanted was to see a movie, not feel as if I had been in one," he said.

"Don't worry, Eddie," Kate said. "I'll be right there. It will be okay."

Eddie sat down and waited for Kate. "She is quite a catch," he said to himself. "When she comes to fetch me, I am going to thank her and hug her tight."

1 Read and Write. Use the rules you know to read the new words.

| gas
pass | **1.** Knowing that he needed _____ at once, Ben didn't _____ any cars. |

| numb
thumb | **2.** Sandy said that her _____ was _____ after she put ice on her cut. |

| one
none
done | **3.** _____ of the women had to bake any cakes for the party since _____ man had _____ all the baking. |

| knew
new
few | **4.** Min-hee _____ that a _____ of the women at the party were _____ in town. |

| lights
right
night | **5.** Aunt Louise was _____ when she said that having all the _____ on would help Jack stay awake at _____ while he worked on his taxes. |

| see
knee
fee | **6.** Eddie could _____ that he would have to pay quite a big _____ to have the cut on his _____ and the car fixed. |

| note
wrote
vote | **7.** Andy _____ a _____ to Roy in which he asked him to _____ for Tom at the meeting. |

| neck
wreck
heck | **8.** "What the _____," said Eddie." I should be happy that I didn't hurt my _____ in the _____." |

| locked
dock
knock | **9.** Aunt Louise had left her keys down at the _____ and was _____ out. She had to _____ ten times, and then Kate came to let her in. |

| day
way
lay | **10.** When Ms. Bond _____ down last night, she hoped that she could find her _____ downtown by herself the next _____. |

2 Opposites. Pick the word that means the opposite, and write it on the line.

| back
bad | huge
last | night
play | sad
same | there
wrong |

___night___   **1.** day   _____ **6.** little

_____ **2.** first   _____ **7.** right

_____ **3.** front   _____ **8.** work

_____ **4.** good   _____ **9.** here

_____ **5.** happy   _____ **10.** opposite

3 Word Study. Pick the word that does not fit with the rest, and write it on the line.

1. Monday   Friday   Thursday   yesterday   <u>yesterday</u>

2. aunt   dad   friend   mom   _____

3. bus   cab   car   foot   _____

4. ant   cat   donkey   monkey   _____

5. day   sun   week   year   _____

6. boy   females   guy   man   _____

7. buns   cakes   candy   wine   _____

8. crying   fussy   mad   numb   _____

9. cot   home   hut   tent   _____

10. fit   hat   pants   robe   _____

The *r*-Controlled Vowels

ar:	car	card	arm	harm	dark	chart	
are:	care	bare	dare	fare	rare	scared	
or:	more	morning	store	wore	fortune	fork	sort
er:	her	herd	jerk	nerve	serve	verse	
eer:	beer	deer	jeer	peer			
ir:	girl	dirt	skirt	birthday	birth	firm	firmly
ur:	hurt	turn	burn	curve	curtain	purse	surf

Words for Study

ad	I've	held	Mary	boyfriend
teller	address	inside	tell	act
silly	stopped	lose	palm	laughed

The Fortune-Teller

Aunt Louise and Kate were out walking on Sunday morning. They were trying to think of something fun to do.

"I know," said Kate, taking a card out of her purse. "Last week, a girl handed me this card."

Aunt Louise peered at the card in Kate's hand. It was an ad for a fortune-teller.

"I think it could be a lot of fun," Kate said. "We never do that sort of thing."

"I don't know," said Aunt Louise. "It seems a bit silly. But if you want to go, we can."

"I've wanted to get my fortune told, but I've never had the nerve," Kate said. "It's the sort of thing that Eddie would jeer at. He dared me to go once, but I didn't. I think if you were with me, I would not feel scared."

"Okay," said Aunt Louise. "There is no harm in trying something new."

Kate and Aunt Louise walked to the address on the card. Kate stopped outside, but Aunt Louise held her arm and walked inside.

"Don't lose your nerve, Kate," she said firmly.

Inside, the store seemed dark. A woman walked out from behind a curtain. She wore a long skirt and lots of rings. She said her name was Mary and asked how she could help them.

"Kate, here, would like her fortune told," said Aunt Louise.

Mary turned to Kate. "I can look at your cards. Or, if you tell me your birthday, I can look at your chart. I can also look at your palm."

Kate held out her palm. The women sat down in the back of the store. Mary held Kate's bare hand firmly and peered at the lines on her palm.

"You will live a long, happy life," Mary said. "Your boyfriend loves you, but he will act like a jerk if you tell him about this."

"You are so right about Eddie!" Kate laughed. "Tell me more!"

1 Read and Write. Add -er to these words.

1. quick + er = __quicker__   **4.** box + er = _____

2. tight + er = _____   **5.** hunt + er = _____

3. tell + er = _____   **6.** herd + er = _____

1. fine + er = __finer__   **4.** bake + er = _____

2. rude + er = _____   **5.** late + er = _____

3. cute + er = _____   **6.** dine + er = _____

1. big + er = __bigger__   **4.** win + er = _____

2. fat + er = _____   **5.** hit + er = _____

3. hot + er = _____   **6.** mug + er = _____

2 Read and Write. More words that end in *-er*.

bumper (bǔmp-er)

1. On Saturday morning, Tim fixed the _____ on his car.

hammer (hăm-mer)

2. He used a _____ to hit it firmly.

copper (cǒp-per)

3. _____ is used to make some pots and pans.

summer (sǔm-mer)

4. Min-hee is saving her money to go to Cape Cod for the _____.

pepper (pěp-per)

5. Dave put red _____ on his rice to make it hotter.

ruler (rūl-er)

6. Mack didn't have a _____, so he could not get the lines right.

worker (work-er)

7. The new _____ was just hired yesterday.

better (bět-ter)

8. The _____ Bob did his job, the _____ he liked his job.

3 Read and Write. Change the *y* to *i* and add *-er*.

handy _____   lovely _____

happy _____   fussy _____

lucky _____   bumpy _____

Use the words ending in *-ier* for these sentences.
New word: than

1. Dan was _____ in getting a ride to work than he thought he would be.

2. Mr. Jones was much _____ once his taxes were out of the way.

3. He said to his wife, "You look _____ than you did on the day I first met you."

4. The baby was _____ when she woke up from her morning nap.

5. "Don't you think this lane is a lot _____ than it was last summer?" Ms. Bond asked her friend.

6. Bob was a lot _____ when he was fixing bikes than when he was fixing cars.

4 Read and Write. Who does what?

a banker	a hunter	a surfer
a catcher	a joker	a thinker
a fighter	a singer	a writer

_____ **1.** Who uses a gun to get deer?

_____ **2.** Who uses a pen?

_____ **3.** Who rides the waves?

_____ **4.** Who knows a lot of songs?

_____ **5.** Who kids around a lot and likes to make you laugh?

_____ **6.** Who keeps your money for you or lends you some money when you need it?

_____ **7.** Who boxes in a ring and hopes he is not knocked out?

_____ **8.** Who gets the ball?

_____ **9.** Who uses his mind and has lots of thoughts?

Vowel Combinations

aide

āi	ea	ea	ie	oa	ue
āid *male*	eat	dead	die	boat	due
paid	meat	head	lie	soap	dues
mail	tea	lead	pie	coat	Sue
rain	clean	read	tie	goal	blue
wait	read			load	true

oi	oo	oo	ou
oil	food	foot	loud
boil	mood	book	loudly
join	room	cook	house
joint	soon	look	count
voice	zoo	wood	shout

Words for Study

gotten	you're	celebrate	well
kiss	temper	hear	aren't
water	that's	sorry	enough

The Fight

Kate was a happy woman, but she was in a bad mood today. She had not gotten any mail for a week. She needed a new coat, but she didn't have the money to buy one. The house was a mess, but she didn't feel like cleaning it.

Kate fixed herself a cup of tea and waited for Eddie. He was due very soon. What would Eddie think of the messy house? Kate didn't care. Eddie's home was a mess all the time. So Kate thought it was all right if her house looked messy now and then.

Then Eddie came into the room. He was so happy that he was humming a tune in a very loud voice. He was just about to kiss Kate when he saw how messy the room looked and how sad Kate was.

He stopped humming and said, "You do know what soap and water are for, don't you? And why are you in a bad mood?"

Kate counted to ten and then shouted, "Look, if you're going to pick a fight, you can go right back home. I am in no mood to put up with your bad temper right now."

Eddie said, "Okay. I'm going over to Bob's house. Maybe he will celebrate my new job with me."

"A new job!" said Kate. "Eddie, I'm sorry I lost my temper. I don't know what's gotten into me."

"That's okay. I'm too happy to be mad. Come on, let's celebrate and go out to eat," said Eddie.

"I can't wait to hear about the job," Kate said. "And, again, I'm so sorry I shouted at you."

"Sorry enough to pay for the dinner?" joked Eddie.

"Well," Kate said, "not that sorry."

1 Read and Write. Fill in the blank with the right word.

boiled	fork	mug	tea
eat	house	night	water
five	meat	soap	work

It was _____ o'clock, and Kate had gotten home from _____. Aunt Louise had been over to Jack's _____ for dinner.

Kate knew she would feel better after she had something to _____. She got out some _____ that was left over from last night and _____ some water for tea. She put the _____ in a _____ and ate the meat with a _____.

When she was done, she soaked all the things she had used in _____ and _____ and went over to Min-hee's house for the _____.

2 Read and Write.

deer *or* peer

1. The men hunted for _____ all day. When they could not find any, they gave up and went home.

read *or* road

2. The _____ was so bumpy that five men had to be hired to fix it.

die *or* due

3. The rent was _____ in one week.

car *or* far

4. Mr. Jones knew he was lost, but he said, "Well, I came this _____. I can't quit looking for the right street now."

barn *or* burn

5. Sue wanted to know who had let the hens out of the _____.

aids *or* ails

6. Eddie said to Kate, "What _____ you?"

lead *or* load

7. "Aren't you going to help me take this _____ of junk to the dump?" asked Mrs. Jones. "It's too much for me to do alone."

pies *or* peas

8. Aunt Louise got out a can of _____ to serve with the meat for dinner.

soak *or* seek

9. Do you _____ your feet in hot water when they hurt?

mood *or* moon

10. It was late, but Jack used the light of the _____ to find his key.

pain *or* paid

11. The _____ in Mike's head was so bad that he wanted to cry.

foot *or* food

12. Eddie put his _____ on the gas too quickly and banged into the car in front of him.

mood *or* maid

13. Kate looked at her messy house and said, "If only I had a _____."

read *or* real

14. Dave was a _____ fighter, but he would only fight if he had to.

house *or* mouse

15. Mr. Jones cried out when he saw a little _____ run right over his foot.

coals *or* coat

16. The _____ died down, and the fire went out.

mail *or* main

17. Ms. Hope didn't like living on the _____ street in her town.

card *or* cared

18. None of us _____ that the boys were playing in the dirt.

bored *or* bared

19. Aunt Louise thought that since life had been so good to her, she had no right to feel _____.

hard *or* herd

20. Do you think this work is _____?

3 Read and Write.

1. Do you like it better when the sun is out or when the moon is out?

_____

2. Do you think that movies are boring, or do you like going to them now and then?

_____

3. When you ride on the bus, do you like to sit in the front or the back?

_____

4. Can you keep a tune, or do you sing off-key?

_____

5. Do you write with your right hand or your left hand?

_____

6. When the roads are icy, do you go out or do you stay at home?

_____

7. Do you eat first thing in the morning, or do you wait until you have been up for a while?

_____

8. Do you lose your temper when things seem to go wrong, or do you try to stay relaxed?

_____

9. Do you think that knowing how to read helps you or hurts you in setting your goals?

_____

Word Index: Lessons 1-12

A

a
about
ace
act
ad
add
address
after
again
age
ago
aid
ail
all
all right
alone
also
am
amuse
amusement
an
and
Andy
ant
any
are
aren't
arm
around
as
ask
at
ate
aunt
awake
away
awoke

B

baby
back
bad
bake
ball
band
bang
bank
banker
bare
barn
bat
batch
be
Becky
bed
beef
been
beep
beer
beet
behind
Ben
bent
bet
better
bid
big
bike
bind
birth
birthday
bit
bite
blue
boat
Bob
boil
bomb
bond
bone
bony
book
bore
box
boy
boyfriend
breath
buck
bud
bug
bum
bump
bumper
bumpy
bun
bunk
bunt
burn
bus
but
buy
by

C

cab
cage
cake
call
came
camp
can
candy
cane
can't
cap
cape
Cape Cod
car
card
care
case
casino
cat
catch
catcher
celebrate
cell phone
cent
chart
check
clean
climb
clock
coal
coat
cod
code
Coke
come
cone
cook
cop
cope
copper
cot
could
count
cry
cub
cube
cup
curtain
curve
cut
cute

D

dab
dad
dam
damp
Dan
Danny
dare
dark
date
Dave
day
dead
deck
deer
den
dent
dice
Dick
did
didn't
die
dig
dime
dine
dinner
dirt
dirty
ditch
dive
do
dock
done
donkey
don't
dope
dot
down
downtown
doze
duck
due
dues
dug
duke
dumb
dump
dune
dunk
Dutch

E

eat
Eddie
eel
end
enough

F

face
fact
fad
fade
fake
fame
fan
fang
far
fare
fat
fed
fee
feed
feel
feet
female
fetch
few
fifty
fig
fight
fighter
file
find
fine
fire
firm
firmly
first
fit
five
fix
fond
food
foot
for
fork
fortune
fortune-teller
forty
fox
Friday
friend
friendly
from
front
fume
fun
fund(s)
funk
funny
fuse
fuss
fussy

G

game
gas
gate
gave
get
girl
girlfriend
go
goal
gong
good
got
gotten
green
gum
gun
guy

H

had
ham
hammer
hand
handy
hang
happy
hard
harm
has
hat
hate
have
he
head
hear
heck
heel
held
help
hen
her
herd
here
herself
hid
hide
hike
him
himself
hint
hip
hire
his
hit
hock
hole
home
honk
hop
hope
horn
hose

hot
house
how
hug
huge
hum
hung
hunt
hunter
hurt
hut

I

I
ice
icy
idea
if
I'll
I'm
in
ink
inside
into
is
it
itch
it's
I've

J

jab
Jack
jack
jam
jazz
jeep
jeer
jerk
job
join
joint
joke
joker
Jones
jot
joy
jug
jump

June
junk
just

K

Kate
keel
keep
ketchup
key
kick
kid
kind
king
kiss
kit
kite
knee
knew
knife
knock
knot
know
known

L

lab
lace
lack
lake
lamb
lame
lamp
land
lane
lap
laptop
last
late
laugh
lay
lead
led
left
lend
lent
less
let
let's

lick
lid
lie
life
light
like
lime
limp
line
lint
little
live
load
lobby
lock
lone
long
look
lose
lost
lot(s)
loud
loudly
Louise
love
lovely
loyal
luck
lucky
lug
lung

M

Mack
mad
made
maid
mail
main
make
male
man
Mary
mat
match
mate
may
maybe
me

meat
meet
meeting
men
mend
mess
messy
met
mice
might
Mike
mile
mind
mine
Min-hee
mint
minute
miss
mitt
mix
mob
mock
mole
mom
Monday
money
monkey
mood
moon
mop
more
morning
mouse
movie
Mr.
Mrs.
Ms.
much
mud
muddy
mug
muggy
mule
muse
mute
my
myself

N

name
nap
neck
need
needy
nerve
net
never
new
next
nice
nick
night
nine
ninety
no
nod
none
nope
nose
nosy
not
note
now
nude
numb
nut
nutty

O

o'clock
of
off
oil
okay
on
once
one
online
only
opposite
or
out
outside
oven
over

P

pace
pack
pad
page
paid
pain
pale
palm
pan
pant
pants
park
party
pass
pat
patch
pay
payday
payment
pea
peck
peek
peel
peer
pen
pep
pepper
pet
phone
pick
pie
pig
pile
pin
pine
pink
play
please
pod
poke
pole
pond
pop
pot
problem
punt
purse
put

Q

quack
quick
quickly
quit
quite

R

race
rack
rage
rain
rake
ram
ramp
ran
rang
rank
rare
rat
rate
read
real
red
reel
refund
refuse
relax
remind
rent
rice
rid
ride
rig
right
ring
rip
ripe
road
rob
robe
rock
rod
rode
role
room
rope
rose

rot
Roy
royal
rub
rude
rug
rule
ruler
run
rung
runt

S

sack
sad
safe
safely
said
sale
same
sand
Sandy
sandy
sang
sank
sat
Saturday
save
saw
say
scared
see
seed
seek
seem
seen
seep
send
sent
serve
set
she
should
shout
sick
side
sight
silly
since

sing
singer
sink
sip
sit
six
sixty
skirt
sky
so
soak
soap
sob
sock
some
something
song
soon
sorry
sort
spend
spent
stay
stomach
stop
store
street
sub
suds
Sue
sum
summer
sun
Sunday
sung
sunk
sunny
surf
surfer

T

tab
tack
take
tale
talk
tame
tan
tank

tap
tax
tea
tell
teller
temper
ten
tent
than
thank
that
that's
the
them
then
there
they
thing
think
thinker
this
thought
thumb
Thursday
tick
tide
tie
tight
tile
Tim
time
tin
tire
to
today
told
Tom
tone
too
top
town
toy
true
try
tub
tube
Tuesday
tug
tune

turn

U

until
up
us
use

V

van
verse
very
voice
vote

W

wade
wage
wait
wake
walk
want
was
wasn't
watch
water
wave
way
we
web
wed
Wednesday
weed
week
weekly
weep
well
went
were
wet
what
what's
when
where
which
while
who
why
wide

wife
wig
will
win
wind
wine
wing
wink
wipe
wire
wiry
witch
with
without
woke
woman
women
won
won't
wood
word
wore
work
worker
worry
would
wrap
wreck
wrist
write
writer
wrong
wrote

X

Y

year
yes
yesterday
yet
you
your
you're

Z

zip
zone
zoo

The *r*-Controlled Vowel Combinations

air:	air	fair	hair	pair	stair
ear:	ear	dear	hear	near	year
ear:	bear	pear	tear	wear	swear
oar:	oar	roar	board		
oor:	door	doorway	poor	floor	
our:	our	hour	sour	flour	
our:	four	pour	court	course	

A Review of Sounds

car	**dark**	**part**	**paid**	**mail**
bar	bark	art	aid	fail
far	lark	cart	laid	jail
jar	mark	smart	maid	nail
tar	park	start	raid	tail
eat	**clean**	**saw**	**now**	**cool**
beat	bean	jaw	bow	fool
heat	jeans	law	cow	pool
neat	lean	paw	how	tool
seat	mean	raw	wow	school

Words for Study

class	high	their	forget
during	learn	picture	really
television	paint	worse	diner
evenings	teacher	felt	Joan

Night School

Dave had made up his mind to take a class at night school. He was getting tired of just going to work during the day. He was also tired of looking at television, hanging out with his friends, or seeing Min-hee in the evenings.

Dave had failed art in high school, but he really wanted to learn to paint. Maybe with the aid of a good teacher, he could pick up some hints on how to paint better.

On his first night, the teacher told them that their first class was going to be a picture of a pear. Dave worked for about an hour on his picture. He knew his picture didn't look like a pear at all. It looked more like a jar. He put a dab of paint here and a dab of paint there, but this only made his picture look worse.

Dave felt like a fool. He wanted to tear the picture up and forget all about night school.

Then a lovely woman, who was painting near Dave, said, "Wow, that really looks like a pear! How did you learn to paint like that?" Dave saw that the pear in her picture looked like a box.

Dave lied, "I have been painting for years. Your picture is good, too. Would you like to go to the diner down the street with me when we are done? I would like to buy you a Coke. We can talk about painting."

"What a good idea!" the woman said. "I would love to. By the way, my name is Joan. What's your name?"

"Dave," said Dave. He wanted to look cool, so he went back to painting his pear. His painting didn't look so bad to him now. Night school was going to be a lot more fun than he thought it would be.

1 Read and Write. Use a word from the box for each sentence in the set.

soon
moon
noon

1. Did you see the _____ last night?

2. Bob said that he would meet Eddie at _____.

3. It would _____ be time for Kate to take the cake out of the oven.

maid
mail
main

4. Sue hoped there was a birthday card from her mom and dad in the _____.

5. The _____ act at the zoo was a bear and her four cubs.

6. Bob hired a _____ to come in once a week to clean his house.

card
cart
carve

7. Andy needed a better knife to _____ the beef.

8. When Aunt Louise bumped into the _____ in the parking lot, she hurt her arm.

9. Kate could not make up her mind which _____ she wanted to buy for Eddie.

meat
meal
mean

10. Tom fed his pet raw _____ for dinner.

11. Mr. and Mrs. Jones eat their main _____ at six o'clock.

12. The little girl was so _____ that she didn't have any friends.

code
cone
cope

13. Joan wrote the zip _____ on the card she sent her dad.

14. When Bob can't _____ with all the work, he gets a friend to help him.

15. Min-hee picked up a pine _____ at the park and put it in her purse.

more
sore
tore
wore

16. Dave _____ up his picture as soon as he got home.

17. Aunt Louise's arm was so _____ that she could not go to work for a week.

18. Mike _____ his new pants to the party Friday night.

19. Kids are _____ than happy when school is out for the summer.

lead
lean
leaf
leak

20. Min-hee didn't know that her gas tank had a _____ in it.

21. Eddie liked _____ meat better than meat with a lot of fat in it.

22. The _____ singer in the band called in sick Tuesday night.

23. Sandy knew it was time to turn over a new _____.

| horn |
| corn |
| born |
| torn |
| worn |

24. Bob was _____ out from working so hard.

25. Eddie honked the _____ four times, but Kate said that she didn't hear it.

26. Jack fixed ham and _____ for his evening meal.

27. The rug was so _____ up from the cat that Ben had to buy a new one.

28. The baby was _____ at one o'clock in the morning.

2 Read and Write. More work with the ending -er.

boarder	helper	teacher
catcher	keeper	teller
diner	painter	voter

_____ **1.** Who would like the art classes at night school?

_____ **2.** Who takes care of the monkeys at the zoo?

_____ **3.** Who uses a mitt?

_____ **4.** Who lives in your home and pays you for rent and food?

_____ **5.** Who picks the men and women who want to run your town?

_____ **6.** Who likes to go out to eat a lot?

_____ **7.** Who gave you aid when you had a problem?

_____ **8.** Who hopes you like doing this page of work?

_____ **9.** Who helps you take money out of the bank?

3 Word Study. Pick the word that does not fit with the rest, and write it on the line.

1. ear   head   lip   nose   _____

2. evening   morning   noon   year   _____

3. beets   corn   pear   peas   _____

4. ace   dice   king   joker   _____

5. bake   boil   cook   oven   _____

6. air   beer   tea   water   _____

7. candy   food   gum   mints   _____

8. can   jar   jug   tea   _____

9. fake   real   right   true   _____

10. dues   fee   taxes   wages   _____

11. green   blue   pink   dark   _____

12. bumper   car   van   jeep   _____

4 Read and Write. Mark the vowels.

1. ădd

2. bīt¢

3. gate

4. damp

5. send

6. clock

7. pop

8. same

9. fume

10. reel

11. hike

12. hunt

13. doze

14. dunk

15. zone

16. deck

Vowels Followed by the Letter *l*

al:	ball	bald	hall	fall	mall	tall	false	salt
el:	belt	melt	held	help	fell	bell	yell	self
il:	ill	bill	hill	fill	milk	pill	spill	
ild:	mild	wild	child					
ol:	old	cold	gold	told	bolt	roll		
ul:	dull	bulb	pulse					
ull:	full	pull	bull					

Words for Study

opened	most	eyes	computer
must	almost	according	deal
stories	always	month	least
however	hi	mistake	give

Paying Bills

Eddie stopped by Jack's house on his way home from work. He wanted Jack to see the new cell phone that he got on sale at the mall. Jack said Eddie was never home when he called. Now they could talk all the time.

When Eddie opened the front door, he could hear Jack laughing loudly in the den. Eddie stayed in the hall for a minute. It was good to hear Jack laugh. "He must be reading that book Aunt Louise lent him," thought Eddie to himself. She had told Jack that he would get a big kick out of the writer's funny stories.

However, when Eddie walked into the den, he saw that Jack wasn't reading the book. In fact, he was doing what he hated the most. Jack was paying his bills.

Now, Jack was a mild man who almost never lost his temper. But bills and taxes always made him wild. All of Jack's friends knew to stay away when he was paying his bills. Jack would swear a little, yell a lot, and just about pull his hair out. At the rate Jack was going, he was lucky that he wasn't bald yet.

"Jack," said Eddie, "you're not ill, are you?"

"Hi, Eddie," laughed Jack. "It's good to see you. Have a seat." Jack was laughing so hard that his eyes were filled with tears.

"Are you going to tell me what's so funny?" asked Eddie.

Jack handed Eddie his phone bill. When Eddie saw it, he started laughing, too. According to the bill, Jack's payment for the month was only ten cents. "Wow, what a mistake!" said Eddie. "The computer really gave you a good deal this month. What are you going to do?"

"Why, I'm going to give them a dime, of course," laughed Jack. "Paying bills is so dull and boring that I might as well have a little fun this time. How do you feel about paying bills?"

Eddie thought for a minute and then said, "Well, I'm so happy that I have a job that I don't mind paying bills right now. It feels good to have the money to pay them."

"That's not a bad idea," said Jack. "Maybe I should try to look at paying bills that way, too."

"You should," laughed Eddie. "At least it might keep you from going bald."

1 Read and Write. Add -ful to the words, and then put them on the right lines.

harm + ful = _____	care + ful = _____
help + ful = _____	use + ful = _____
watch + ful = _____	thank + ful = _____

1. When Eddie saw that Jack was paying bills, he tried to be _____.

2. Aunt Louise worries about Eddie and keeps a _____ eye on him.

3. Eddie thought he should stay out of the _____ sun.

4. Eddie could think of a lot of ways that his new cell phone would be _____.

5. Jack was _____ that he had a good friend like Eddie.

6. Jack and Eddie learned to be more _____ with their money.

2 Read and Write. Add *-less* to the words, and then put them on the right lines.

harm + less = _____   breath + less = _____

help + less = _____   care + less = _____

hope + less = _____   time + less = _____

1. Aunt Louise said the songs at the amusement park were _____.

2. The ride she went on with Jack left her _____.

3. She was _____ with her purse and left it in a bumper car.

4. Aunt Louise thought looking for it was _____ and that she would not get it back.

5. Jack felt _____. He didn't know what to do.

6. Aunt Louise was scared to talk to the man at the ride. But Jack said he was _____.

3 Read and Write. Match the words that mean the same thing.

bare	dead	hurt	poor	soaked
carve	handy	ill	shout	street

_____ **1.** cut

_____ **2.** sick

_____ **3.** useful

_____ **4.** road

_____ **5.** all wet

_____ **6.** yell

_____ **7.** harm

_____ **8.** nude

_____ **9.** needy

_____ **10.** not living

4 Read and Write. Match the words that mean the opposite.

cold	false	inside	never	take
dumb	harmless	messy	start	worse

_____ **1.** hot

_____ **2.** stop

_____ **3.** outside

_____ **4.** better

_____ **5.** give

_____ **6.** neat

_____ **7.** always

_____ **8.** true

_____ **9.** smart

_____ **10.** harmful

5 Read and Write. Use a word from **A** and a word from **B** to fill in the lines.

A	B
all	beds
art	bus
bear	cake
birthday	canes
bunk	class
candy	✓coat
car	cub
cell	keys
dining	lot
✓lab	phone
parking	right
school	room
soap	suds

1. Dr. Chase always wore a __lab__ __coat__.

2. After I saw Dr. Chase, I knew I would be _____ _____.

3. The girls were licking red _____ _____.

4. I put the dirty cat in a tub full of _____ _____.

5. The kids had _____ _____ in their room.

6. Eddie saw a wild _____ _____ in the woods.

7. He has a picture of it on his _____ _____.

8. This morning I could not find my _____ _____.

9. When I got to work there was no room in the _____ _____.

10. Aunt Louise baked Kate a _____ _____.

11. She put the cake in the _____ _____.

12. The _____ _____ was very late today.

13. I didn't get to _____ _____ on time.

Digraphs and Consonant Blends

ch			**sh**		
chase	cheap	choose	shook	shock	shine
chair	chest		shop	shut	short
each		rich	show	shape	
reach	church	lunch		fish	rush
much	such	search	cash	wish	flush

st			**sk**		
stop	step	still	skate	skin	skill
stale	storm	stuff	skirt	skunk	sky
stare	strike	fist			
east	west	list	ask	task	desk
fast	toast	burst	mask	risk	dusk

Words for Study

Internet	odd	Elvis	guess
auction	people	other	proud
easy	selling	slammed	owner
screen	piece	oh	couldn't

Kate Shops Online

It was Saturday morning, and Eddie and Kate were surfing the Internet. "Eddie, do you think it is too much of a risk to shop online?" asked Kate. "I need to buy a cheap chair, and I thought I could check an online auction."

Eddie loved to shop online. He got stuff from online auctions all the time. "It's easy and safe," he said. "You don't have to worry about cash, and you don't have to step outside! Let me show you."

Eddie opened a web page. The computer screen filled up with stuff for sale. There were chairs, desks, chests, and all sorts of stuff.

Kate saw some skates and a skirt she wanted to buy. She wished she were rich so she could choose all the things she wanted. But after looking at lots of stuff, she only got a cheap chair.

"See, wasn't that easy?" Eddie asked. "Now that you got your chair, let's have some fun. We can see what sorts of odd things people are selling."

Eddie and Kate searched the list. "Look," Kate said, "that guy is selling a piece of toast shaped like Elvis! Who would buy such a silly thing?" She stared at the page in shock. The bidding was up to $100 for a piece of stale toast!

"I wish I could sell some of my lunch and strike it rich," she said. Eddie burst out laughing.

Kate didn't see what was so funny. She was feeling short-tempered. "All I can buy is a cheap chair, when other people are wasting so much money!" she said. She slammed her fist down on the desk. Her hand hit one of the computer keys.

"Oh no, Kate!" Eddie said. "You hit 'Buy Now'! I guess you are the proud owner of a piece of Elvis toast!"

"I thought you said that shopping online was safe, Eddie," Kate yelled, her face flushed. "I'm never going to ask you to help me shop online again."

She stormed out of the room and slammed the door shut. Eddie shook his head. He couldn't stop laughing.

1 Read and Write. Add -est to these words.

1. near + est = __nearest__   **4.** smart + est = _____

2. cheap + est = _____   **5.** short + est = _____

3. rich + est = _____

1. fine + est = __finest__   **4.** ripe + est = _____

2. safe + est = _____   **5.** late + est = _____

3. rude + est = _____

1. big + est = __biggest__   **4.** mad + est = _____

2. hot + est = _____   **5.** sad + est = _____

3. fat + est = _____

2 Read and Write. Change the *y* to *i* and add *-est*.

funny + est = <u>funniest</u>   lucky + est = _____

happy + est = _____   dirty + est = _____

easy + est = _____

1. What is the _____ way to get downtown?

2. The kids got _____ from playing in the mud.

3. Only the _____ people win huge sums of money.

4. Mary was _____ when she was out surfing.

5. Andy was the <u>funniest</u> man at the party.

3 Read and Write. Match the words that mean the same thing.

auction	easy	people	slam	tug
chair	must	piece	torn	wish

_____ **1.** hope for   _____ **6.** sale

_____ **2.** not hard   _____ **7.** seat

_____ **3.** ripped   _____ **8.** hit

_____ **4.** pull   _____ **9.** men, women, and kids

_____ **5.** part   _____ **10.** have to

4 Read and Write. Choose the right word, and write it on the line.

stop *or* stuff	**1.** Dave didn't know why people would want to buy _____ online.
add *or* odd	**2.** To him, it seemed _____ that they would not go shop at a store.
stare *or* store	**3.** Dave hated to _____ at a computer screen for very long.
cash *or* case	**4.** Online stores won't let you pay in _____.
numb *or* dumb	**5.** Eddie loved to buy stuff online. He thought people who didn't like the Internet were _____.
fuss, fat, *or* fast	**6.** Shopping online was also _____. Dave liked to get done quickly.
much, such, *or* lunch	**7.** There was so _____ stuff for sale online. Dave had a hard time choosing what to buy.
church, cheap, *or* check	**8.** Eddie said he had gotten lots of _____ stuff online.
desk *or* dusk	**9.** Eddie didn't mind sitting at a _____ for hours at a time.
well, tell, *or* sell	**10.** "People _____ some really odd stuff online," Eddie told Dave.
fish, wish, *or* dish	**11.** Dave said, "I _____ I could sell some of my things online."
search *or* such	**12.** "That's a good idea!" Eddie said. "Let's _____ and see what sells well."

Consonant Blends

bl:	blame	black	bleed	bless	blind	block
cl:	clear	clip	close	clothes	cloth	club
fl:	flame	flat	flock	flour	flush	fly
gl:	glass	glad	gland	glare	gleam	glue
pl:	place	plate	plane	plan	plug	plus
sl:	slam	sleep	sleeve	slice	slip	slow

Words for Study

badly	nobody	Baker	haven't
faint	nurse	many	rest
Dr.	goodness	loveliest	death
middle	does	ever	before
spite	heart	surprised	often

Love

Bob was in such a rush to get to work Friday morning that he slammed his hand in the car door. Almost at once, his hand started to turn black and blue. He picked up an old cloth that was on the floor of his car and wrapped it quickly around his hand. He saw that his thumb was cut. It was bleeding so badly that the cloth was soon red. Bob felt as if he were going to faint.

It was Bob's luck that Dr. Chase's place was in the middle of the next block. In spite of the pain, Bob ran as fast as he could to Dr. Chase's. There was nobody in the waiting room. Then he saw a lovely nurse sitting behind the desk. When she saw Bob's hand, she cried, "My goodness! Does it hurt very much?"

But, by now, Bob wasn't thinking about his hand. He was looking at the nurse, and his heart was beating very fast. The nurse was June Baker. Bob had dated her many years ago when they were in high school. She had been his first true love. Bob had not seen June for six years. She was still the loveliest girl he had ever known.

Then June looked from Bob's hand, which was bleeding all over the rug, to his face. "Why, Bob!" she said in a very surprised voice, "I haven't seen you in ages! Your hand looks bad, but the rest of you looks just fine," she laughed. "It's really good to see you again."

"It's good to see you, too," Bob said. "How about going out with me Saturday night? We can talk about the good old days, and what we are doing now."

"I would love to," said June. "But first, let me get your hand fixed up, so you don't bleed to death before our date."

Bob felt so happy that he thought he would really faint now. Aunt Louise always said, "Bad times can turn into good times a lot more often than people think."

Bob was in all this pain and late for work, yet he had not felt this good for a long, long time.

1 Read and Write. Put the words in the boxes on the right lines.

rip
slip
flip
hip

1. Be careful! If you _____ on the wet floor, you might hurt your _____.

2. Would you please _____ to the last page and _____ it out of the book for me?

male
pale
tales
stale
sale

3. Do nurses turn _____ when they see people bleeding?

4. Dan is buying a _____ cat that is on _____ at the pet shop.

5. We had tea and _____ cake while Aunt Louise told us many funny _____.

jump
dump
lump
bump
pump

6. The van blew a tire when it hit a _____ on the road to the _____.

7. After the rain I had to _____ the water out of my house.

8. Bob fell when he tried to _____ over a ditch on his bike. Now he has a _____ on his arm.

page
rage
age
stage
wage

9. Mark flew into a _____ when he couldn't find his socks.

10. Min-hee makes a very good _____ for a woman her _____.

11. Ever since Sue had the leading role in a high school play, she wanted to be on the _____.

12. From the very first _____, Jack knew that the book was going to amuse him.

pain
rain
plain
stains
Main

13. It was _____ to June that Bob was in a lot of _____.

14. After a week of _____, _____ Street was a mess.

15. Kate came back from lunch with ketchup _____ all over her new top.

name
shame
lame
blamed
same
came

16. Min-hee thought it was a _____ that Mark's cat has a _____ foot.

17. When Joan _____ to the party, we all knew her _____.

18. Joan left her things around the house so often that she never _____ other people when they did the _____ thing.

stare
care
glare
scared
rare

19. The _____ at night made Aunt Louise _____ to get in the car.

20. Kate didn't _____ that Eddie liked to cook his beef _____.

21. It had been so long since I had seen her that all I could do was _____.

blushed
rush
slush

22. Dave had to _____ to get to work on time.

23. The ice and rain had left _____ on the roads.

24. June _____ when she first saw Bob.

chair
hair
fair
stairs
air

25. Mary's _____ was a mess after she fell down the _____.

26. Bob likes to sleep in his new _____.

27. On a _____ day, the _____ is clear.

2 Read and Write. Use a word from **A**, add a word from **B** to it, and fill in the lines.

A	B
check	book
day	cakes
hair	cap
knee	✓check
nick	coat
pan	cut
✓pay	light
pepper	mint
rain	name
rest	room

1. Eddie spent his _____ *paycheck* _____ on a card game.

2. Mary ate a _____ candy cane.

3. Can we make it home before the sun is down and _____ ends?

4. Do you know where the men's _____ is?

5. Bob hurt his _____ when he fell off his bike.

6. Joan wore her new black _____ to work today.

7. I keep my _____ in my purse.

8. Mike likes to eat _____ in the morning.

9. Dave is going to the mall to get a _____.

10. Aunt Louise won't tell us what her _____ was when she was a little girl.

3 Read and Write.

1. Would you like to sleep in a tent near the water or in the woods?

_____

2. Which do you like better, ball games or card games?

_____

3. Do you think your writing is neat, or is it hard to read?

_____

4. At the movies do you like candy bars, popcorn, or mints?

_____

5. Do you go to church on weekends, or do you sleep late?

_____

Word Index: Lessons 1–16

A

a
about
according
ace
act
ad
add
address
after
again
age
ago
aid
ail
air
all
all right
almost
alone
also
always
am
amuse
amusement
an
and
Andy
ant
any
are
aren't
arm
around
art
as
ask
at
ate
auction
aunt
awake
away
awoke

B

baby
back
bad
badly
bake
Baker
bald
ball
band
bang
bank

banker
bar
bare
bark
barn
bat
batch
be
bean
bear
beat
Becky
bed
beef
been
beep
beer
beet
before
behind
bell
belt
Ben
bent
bet
better
bid
big
bike
bill
bind
birth
birthday
bit
bite
black
blame
bleed
bless
blew
blind
block
blue
blush
board
boarder
boat
Bob
boil
bolt
bomb
bond
bone
bony
book
bore
born
bow

box
boy
boyfriend
breath
breathless
buck
bud
bug
bulb
bull
bum
bump
bumper
bumpy
bun
bunk
bunk bed
bunt
burn
burst
bus
but
buy
by

C

cab
cage
cake
call
came
camp
can
candy
cane
can't
cap
cape
Cape Cod
car
card
care
careful
careless
cart
carve
case
cash
casino
cat
catch
catcher
celebrate
cell phone
cent
chair
chart
Chase

chase
cheap
check
checkbook
chest
child
choose
church
class
clean
clear
climb
clip
clock
close
cloth
clothes
club
coal
coat
cod
code
Coke
cold
come
computer
cone
cook
cool
cop
cope
copper
corn
cot
could
couldn't
count
course
court
cow
cry
cub
cube
cup
curtain
curve
cut
cute

D

dab
dad
dam
damp
Dan
Danny
dare
dark

date
Dave
day
daylight
dead
deal
dear
death
deck
deer
den
dent
desk
dice
Dick
did
didn't
die
dig
dime
dine
diner
dining room
dinner
dirt
dirty
dish
ditch
dive
do
dock
does
done
donkey
don't
door
doorway
dope
dot
down
downtown
doze
Dr.
duck
due
dues
dug
duke
dull
dumb
dump
dune
dunk
during
dusk
Dutch

E

each
ear
east
easy
eat
Eddie
eel
Elvis
end
enough
evening
ever
eye

F

face
fact
fad
fade
fail
faint
fair
fake
fall
false
fame
fan
fang
far
fare
fast
fat
fed
fee
feed
feel
feet
fell
felt
female
fetch
few
fifty
fig
fight
fighter
file
fill
find
fine
fire
firm
firmly
first
fish
fist

fit
five
fix
flame
flat
flip
flock
floor
flour
flush
fly
fond
food
fool
foot
for
forget
fork
fortune
fortune-teller
forty
four
fox
Friday
friend
friendly
from
front
full
fume
fun
fund(s)
funk
funny
fuse
fuss
fussy

G

game
gas
gate
gave
get
girl
girlfriend
give
glad
gland
glare
glass
gleam
glue
go
goal
gold
gong
good

goodness
got
gotten
green
guess
gum
gun
guy

H

had
hair
haircut
hall
ham
hammer
hand
handy
hang
happy
hard
harm
harmful
harmless
has
hat
hate
have
haven't
he
head
hear
heart
heat
heck
heel
held
help
helper
helpful
helpless
hen
her
herd
here
herself
hi
hid
hide
high
high school
hike
hill
him
himself
hint
hip
hire
his
hit

hock
hole
home
honk
hop
hope
hopeless
horn
hose
hot
hour
house
how
however
hug
huge
hum
hung
hunt
hunter
hurt
hut

I

I
ice
icy
idea
if
ill
I'll
I'm
in
ink
inside
Internet
into
is
it
itch
it's
I've

J

jab
Jack
jail
jam
jar
jaw
jazz
jeans
jeep
jeer
jerk
Joan
job
join
joint

joke
joker
Jones
jot
joy
jug
jump
June
junk
just

K

Kate
keel
keep
keeper
ketchup
key
kick
kid
kind
king
kiss
kit
kite
knee
kneecap
knew
knife
knock
knot
know
known

L

lab
lace
lack
laid
lake
lamb
lame
lamp
land
lane
lap
laptop
lark
last
late
laugh
law
lay
lead
leaf
leak
lean
learn
least

led
left
lend
lent
less
let
let's
lick
lid
lie
life
light
like
lime
limp
line
lint
lip
list
little
live
load
lobby
lock
lone
long
look
lose
lost
lot(s)
loud
loudly
Louise
love
loveliest
lovely
loyal
luck
lucky
lug
lump
lunch
lung

M

Mack
mad
made
maid
mail
main
make
male
mall
man
many
Mark
mark
Mary
mask

mat
match
mate
may
maybe
me
meal
mean
meat
meet
meeting
melt
men
mend
mess
messy
met
mice
middle
might
Mike
mile
mild
milk
mind
mine
Min-hee
mint
minute
miss
mistake
mitt
mix
mob
mock
mole
mom
Monday
money
monkey
month
mood
moon
mop
more
morning
most
mouse
movie
Mr.
Mrs.
Ms.
much
mud
muddy
mug
muggy
mule
muse
must

mute
my
myself

N

nail
name
nap
near
neat
neck
need
needy
nerve
net
never
new
next
nice
nick
nickname
night
nine
ninety
no
nobody
nod
none
noon
nope
nose
nosy
not
note
now
nude
numb
nurse
nut
nutty

O

oar
o'clock
odd
of
off
often
oh
oil
okay
old
on
once
one
online
only
open
opposite

or
other
our
out
outside
oven
over
owner

P

pace
pack
pad
page
paid
pain
paint
painter
pair
pale
palm
pan
pancake
pant
pants
park
parking lot
part
party
pass
pat
patch
paw
pay
paycheck
payday
payment
pea
pear
peck
peek
peel
peer
pen
people
pep
pepper
peppermint
pet
phone
pick
picture
pie
piece
pig
pile
pill
pin
pine
pink

place
plain
plan
plane
plate
play
please
plug
plus
pod
poke
pole
pond
pool
poor
pop
popcorn
pot
pour
problem
proud
pull
pulse
pump
punt
purse
put

Q

quack
quick
quickly
quit
quite

R

race
rack
rage
raid
rain
raincoat
rake
ram
ramp
ran
rang
rank
rare
rat
rate
raw
reach
read
real
really
red
reel

refund
refuse
relax
remind
rent
rest
restroom
rice
rich
rid
ride
rig
right
ring
rip
ripe
risk
road
roar
rob
robe
rock
rod
rode
role
roll
room
rope
rose
rot
Roy
royal
rub
rude
rug
rule
ruler
run
rung
runt
rush

S

sack
sad
safe
safely
said
sale
salt
same
sand
Sandy
sandy
sang
sank
sat
Saturday

save
saw
say
scared
school
school bus
screen
search
seat
see
seed
seek
seem
seen
seep
self
sell
send
sent
serve
set
shame
shape
she
shine
shock
shook
shop
short
should
shout
show
shut
sick
side
sight
silly
since
sing
singer
sink
sip
sit
six
sixty
skate
skill
skin
skirt
skunk
sky
slam
sleep
sleeve
slice
slip
slow
slush
smart

so
soak
soap
sob
sock
some
something
song
soon
sore
sorry
sort
sour
spend
spent
spill
spite
stage
stain
stair
stale
stare
start
stay
step
still
stomach
stop
store
storm
story
street
strike
stuff
sub
such
suds
Sue
sum
summer
sun
Sunday
sung
sunk
sunny
surf
surfer
surprise
swear

T

tab
tack
tail
take
tale
talk
tall

tame
tan
tank
tap
tar
task
tax
tea
teacher
tear
television
tell
teller
temper
ten
tent
than
thank
thankful
that
that's
the
their
them
then
there
they
thing
think
thinker
this
thought
thumb
Thursday
tick
tide
tie
tight
tile
Tim
time
timeless
tin
tire
to
toast
today
told
Tom
tone
too
tool
top
tore
torn
town
toy
true
try

tub
tube
Tuesday
tug
tune
turn

U

until
up
us
use
useful

V

van
verse
very
voice
vote
voter

W

wade
wage
wait
wake
walk
want
was
wasn't
watch
watchful
water
wave
way
we
wear
web
wed
Wednesday
weed
week
weekend
weekly
weep
well
went
were
west
wet
what
what's
when
where
which
while
who

why
wide
wife
wig
wild
will
win
wind
wine
wing
wink
wipe
wire
wiry
wish
witch
with
without
woke
woman
women
won
won't
wood
word
wore
work
worker
worn
worry
worse
would
wow
wrap
wreck
wrist
write
writer
wrong
wrote

X

Y

year
yell
yes
yesterday
yet
you
your
you're

Z

zip
zone
zoo

More Consonant Blends

br:	brave	brain	bread	bride	broke	brown
cr:	crazy	crash	cream	crime	crown	crumb
dr:	drain	dream	dress	drive	drove	dry
fr:	freeze	free	fresh	French	froze	fry
gr:	grape	gray	grass	green	groom	ground
pr:	pray	pride	prize	print	proud	prune
tr:	tray	train	trail	tree	treat	trip
str:	straw	stream	strike	string	stroke	strong

Words for Study

even	able	steak	cleaner
because	shirt	hadn't	calm
both	took	whole	ready
upset	decide	jacket	anywhere

Bob Has a Problem

It was Saturday morning, and Bob thought
the night would never come. Running into
June at Dr. Chase's was like a dream come
true. Bob was so happy. He didn't even mind
that his hand still hurt. He didn't even mind
that Dan Rose had yelled at him for five
minutes on the phone because Bob wasn't
strong enough to go back to work yet.

Both Dan and Bob knew it would be crazy for
Bob to work on bikes with his hand all wrapped
up. Dan was just upset that his prize worker was out
sick. Bob knew he would be able to go to work by the
middle of next week.

Right now, all Bob wanted to think about was how he was going
to dress for his date with June. He picked out a dark-green shirt
and a pair of light-gray pants. Bob was proud of his clothes. Even
when he was at work, he took pride in how he looked.

Next, he had to decide where to take June. They could drive out to
the Steak House and have a steak dinner with French fries and a
glass of wine. And after that? Maybe they would see a movie or
go for a walk in the park.

Bob told himself to slow down. He hadn't even talked to June,
and he was trying to plan the whole evening without any idea of
what she wanted to do.

He put on his jacket to go downtown and pick up his good coat from the dry cleaners. That would calm him down a bit. It would also make the time go faster.

He was just getting ready to step out the front door when he froze. All his lovely dreams were going to go down the drain! Since Bob had missed work yesterday, he didn't get his check. How could he take June anywhere when he didn't have a dime to his name?

1 Read and Write. Put the words in the boxes on the right lines.

slow
blow
flow
row

1. When Bob told Dan that he would miss a few days of work, it came as quite a _____ to him.

2. Joan wished she could get the water to _____ a lot faster from her sink.

3. The boys were _____ in getting back to the dock because they had only one oar to _____ the boat with.

pride
prizes
price

4. "What was the _____ of your new tools?" asked Bob.

5. Mary was filled with _____ when she won two _____ for her work in art class.

tested
toast
taste

6. Jack fixed himself two slices of _____ for his lunch.

7. The slices didn't _____ hot enough, so he _____ the toaster to see what the problem was.

chest
best
pests
vests

8. When Dan asked Bob if he would be back to work by Tuesday, he said, "I'll try my _____."

9. Eddie's _____ was so big that none of the _____ he tried on fit him right.

10. Which house _____ do you think are worse—ants or mice?

brown
clown
gown

11. The _____ at the amusement park wore a woman's evening _____ with huge _____ dots all over it.

truck
trunk
trust

12. Mr. Jones filled the _____ of his car with junk, but he still had more junk to get rid of.

13. His wife said that she would rent a _____.

14. Mr. Jones said, "I don't know if I _____ you driving a truck all the way out to the dump alone. I know how you drive."

harming
charming
farm

15. Bob knew that he would just be _____ himself if he went back to work too soon.

16. Many people who live in big towns think that life on a _____ must be very _____.

may
hay
prayed
clay

17. Mary made a lovely _____ pot in art class which she thinks her mom _____ want to put in the living room.

18. The farmers _____ that all the _____ did not burn up in the fire last night.

drops
stopped
crops

19. When the first _____ of rain fell, Kate _____ reading her book and ran out to get the clothes that were on the line.

20. The farmers didn't make as much money from their _____ last summer as they thought they would.

gum
plum
drum

21. When Mary asked if she could buy some _____, her dad said, "Why don't you eat a _____? That would be much better for you."

22. Mack hoped his friends would pool their money and buy him a _____ set for his birthday.

2 Read and Write. Choose the words that have to do with a *town* and put them under **Town.** Put the words that have to do with a *school* under **School.** Put the words that have to do with a *farm* under **Farm.** *(Use each word only once.)*

✓barn	classes	desks	parks	stores
bus stops	cows	hay	pigs	street lights
churches	crops	homework	reading	teachers

Town	School	Farm
1. _____	1. _____	1. _barn_____
2. _____	2. _____	2. _____
3. _____	3. _____	3. _____
4. _____	4. _____	4. _____
5. _____	5. _____	5. _____

3 Read and Write.

	Which do you like *best?*	Which do you like *least?*
fish, ham, beef, *or* lamb	1. _____	_____
black, blue, green, *or* pink	2. _____	_____
bears, deer, monkeys, *or* skunks	3. _____	_____
grapes, plums, pears, *or* prunes	4. _____	_____
cake, candy, ice cream, *or* pie	5. _____	_____
Monday, Friday, Saturday, *or* Sunday	6. _____	_____
buses, cabs, planes, *or* trains	7. _____	_____
beer, Coke, milk, *or* tea	8. _____	_____
bankers, painters, singers, *or* teachers	9. _____	_____
movies, parks, television, *or* zoos	10. _____	_____

More Digraphs and Consonant Blends

wh:	whale	wheat	wheel	white	whip
th:	this	that	these	those	
	thick	thin	third	thirty	thirteen
	tooth	teeth	north	south	math
thr:	three	throw	threw	through	
tw:	twelve	twenty	twice	twin	twist
sm:	smash	small	smell	smile	smoke
sn:	snake	snail	sneeze	snore	snow
sp:	space	speak	spoon	spot	spank
sw:	sweet	sweat	swim	swift	switch

Words for Study

mother	cousin	worst	numbers
father	grade	speed	everybody
Billy	sure	toward	calmly
afternoon	later	legs	nothing

A Way with Kids

Mary's mother and father asked Jack if he would watch Billy that Saturday afternoon. They wanted to take Mary to a play. Billy was Mary's cousin. He was staying with them for a few weeks. He was six years old and was in the first grade.

The three were going out the door. Mary's mother said, "Thank you so much for helping us out, Jack. Just be firm with Billy. I'm sure that things will be all right. We will see you later."

Well, it started out to be one of the worst afternoons of Jack's life. He had no sooner closed the front door when Billy smashed him in the chest with a toy. Just as Jack was thinking that Billy might need a good spanking, Billy wheeled his bike into the room at high speed. He headed toward Jack and rolled it right into his legs.

Jack let out a yell because he had twisted his knee yesterday. Now his whole leg was sore. He was about to swear, but then he stopped himself. He thought, "If I lose my temper, things will get worse. Maybe if I speak to him in the right way, things will get better."

"Billy," said Jack. "Have you learned about numbers in math yet?"

Billy said, "Sure, I know all about numbers."

"Good," said Jack. "Now, tell me this. Which number is bigger—
six or three?"

"Six," laughed Billy. "Everybody knows that!"

"Right. You are a smart boy," smiled Jack. "Now I'm over six
feet tall, and you're maybe three feet tall. What do you think
that means?"

Billy may have been a little wild, but he was no fool. He
knew just what Jack was talking about.

When Mary and her father and mother came home
at three-thirty, Billy was sitting calmly on the
floor and playing with his toy trucks. Jack was
watching a movie on television.

"My goodness!" said Mary's mother.
"You sure do have a way with kids. I've
never seen Billy this calm."

"It's nothing," Jack smiled. "You just have to know how to talk to them,
that's all."

1 Read and Write. Put the words in the boxes on the right lines.

<table>
<tr><td>left
lift</td><td>

1. Dave was able to give Min-hee a _____ to work on
   Tuesday.

2. The skunk _____ a smell that lasted for hours.

</td></tr>
<tr><td>gift
shift</td><td>

3. Mary's mother gave Jack a _____ for being so
   kind.

4. Dave hoped he would be switched from the third to the first
   _____ at the shop where he worked.

</td></tr>
</table>

math
bath
path

5. Mary wanted to see the show on television, so she tried to do her _____ homework while she was taking a _____.

6. If Sandy had been able to find the _____, he could have climbed to the top of the hill in less than twenty minutes.

hill
chill
spilled
grilled

7. It took Sandy over an hour to climb to the top of the _____.

8. Mary _____ her ice cream all over her jacket.

9. Do you like meat better when it's baked or _____?

10. Aunt Louise had to _____ the pie, so it would not taste stale the next day.

dare
fare
flares
spare

11. "Don't you _____ walk on this floor," said Eddie. "I just got through mopping it."

12. Ms. Bond didn't have enough money for cab _____, so she took the bus to work.

13. Aunt Louise really wanted to lend her cousin the money, but she couldn't _____ the cash.

14. The men lit _____ so other drivers would see the wreck.

throw
blow
know
snow

15. Do you _____ how fast the wind will _____?

16. I don't want that. Would you _____ it away for me?

17. Billy loves to play in the _____.

**bib
fibs
ribs
crib**

18. Did you ever tell your mother or father _____ when you were a child?

19. The mother took off the baby's _____ and put him in the _____ for his afternoon nap.

20. The man was so thin from not eating right that you could see his _____.

**coast
toast
roast**

21. This morning Joan made _____ with jam.

22. Jack checked to see if the _____ was clear before he hid the gift in the den.

23. Eddie cooked the _____ beef on the grill.

2 Numbers. Read these number words.

one (1)	six (6)	eleven (11)	sixteen (16)
two (2)	seven (7)	twelve (12)	seventeen (17)
three (3)	eight (8)	thirteen (13)	eighteen (18)
four (4)	nine (9)	fourteen (14)	nineteen (19)
five (5)	ten (10)	fifteen (15)	twenty (20)

Write the word for the right sum on each line.

1. eleven plus seven _____

2. nineteen plus one _____

3. twelve plus three _____

4. eight plus seven _____

5. eight plus eight _____

6. seven plus four _____

7. thirteen plus two _____

8. five plus two _____

9. two plus two _____

10. twelve plus one _____

Write the right number word on each line.

_____ **11.** How many days are in a week?

_____ **12.** How many months are in a year?

_____ **13.** How many meals do you eat each day?

_____ **14.** How many tires does a car have?

_____ **15.** What is your lucky number?

_____ **16.** How many cousins do you have?

_____ **17.** How many hours do you sleep each night?

_____ **18.** How old were you when you first drove a car?

_____ **19.** How many times have you fainted in your life?

_____ **20.** According to an old saying, how many lives does a cat have?

3 Read and Write. Use a word from **A,** add a word from **B** to it, and fill in the lines.

A	B
base	ball
bath	book
bed	book
class	burn
cook	corn
down	end
note	room
pop	room
sun	room
week	stairs

1. Dan worked Monday through Friday and had the _____ off.

2. Sue stayed at the lake too long and got a mild _____.

3. "While you're in the _____," shouted Kate to Aunt Louise, "will you check the water in the tub?"

4. "Don't forget your math _____ on Monday," the teacher said.

5. Eddie got two boxes of _____ in the lobby before the movie started.

6. Dave had twin beds in his _____.

7. When Eddie, Dave, and Mike get together, they like to play _____.

8. Aunt Louise does not use a _____ when she makes dinner.

9. Mary could not find a desk because the _____ was full.

10. Jack went _____ to check the meat in the oven.

LESSON 19
Still More Consonant Blends

sc:	scare	scar	scooter	scout	score
scr:	scratch	screech	scream	scrub	scramble
shr:	shrimp	shrink	shrank	shred	shrug
spl:	splash	spleen	splint	splinter	split
spr:	sprain	sprawl	sprint	sprang	spring
squ:	squat	squeeze	squeal	squash	squirrel
str:	strain	straight	struggle	strap	strict
chr:	chrome	chronic	Christmas		

Words for Study

shiny	yourself	swerved	leave
costs	helmet	brakes	sound
handles	suddenly	second	ticket
spotless	across	wondered	sighed

Kate Buys a Scooter

Kate had saved her money for months so she could buy a bike. She was looking around Dan's bike shop when she let out a squeal.

"How much is that scooter?" she asked Bob. She pointed to a shiny, red scooter. What a splash she would make riding that around town!

"It costs more than you have to spend," said Bob. "But you can take it for a test drive if you want. You can always buy it later."

Kate hopped on the scooter. She sat on the seat and squeezed the handles.

"Be careful, Kate," Bob said. "Don't scratch the chrome. I spent hours scrubbing it so it would look spotless. And don't hurt yourself!"

Kate strapped on a helmet and stepped on the gas. The scooter screeched to a start, heading toward the park. The speed scared Kate. She struggled to keep the scooter straight. Suddenly, a squirrel ran across the street. Kate screamed. She was going to squash it! She shut her eyes and swerved. The brakes squealed loudly. In a split second, Kate lay sprawled in the street.

Bob saw the whole thing. He sprang up and sprinted over to Kate. "Are you okay?" he asked. Kate opened her eyes.

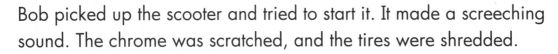

"I'm so sorry, Bob," she said. "Did I hit that poor squirrel?"

Bob shrugged. "No," he said, "it must have scrambled out of the way. But what about your knee? It's bleeding!"

"I think it's sprained," Kate said. She looked at the cut and wondered if it would leave a scar.

Bob picked up the scooter and tried to start it. It made a screeching sound. The chrome was scratched, and the tires were shredded.

A cop pulled up and stepped out of his car. He put a splint on Kate's knee. Then he wrote her a ticket.

"Kate, I'm sorry, but you're going to have to pay for the scooter," Bob said. "Dan is strict about that sort of thing. But, I can fix it for you."

"I'll have to save up a lot of money," sighed Kate. "But at least I didn't squash that squirrel."

1 Read and Write. Choose the right word, and write it on the line.

wrist, list, *or* fist

1. Kate also sprained her _____ when she fell off the scooter.

split, splinter, *or* splint

2. She had to wear a _____ for a few weeks.

scared, scar, *or* scratch

3. At first, she was too _____ to get back on the scooter.

handle, helmet, *or* hammer

4. She made sure to always wear her _____ when she went riding.

screeches, scrubs, *or* scratches

5. Bob fixed the scooter and got all the _____ out of the chrome.

squeal, squat, *or* squash	**6.** Kate was very glad she didn't _____ the squirrel.
spotless *or* harmless	**7.** Dan made Bob scrub all the bikes and scooters until they were _____.
squirrels, squeezes, *or* squeals	**8.** Kate wondered why _____ ran across the road so often.
bakes, brakes, *or* backs	**9.** She always slammed on her _____ when she saw one run across the road.
chronic *or* chrome	**10.** After the wreck, Kate had _____ pain in her knee.
screen, spleen, *or* seen	**11.** Bob said he hadn't _____ a crash like that before.
best, test, *or* rest	**12.** He didn't let any other people _____ drive a scooter.

2 Read and Write. Fill in the line with the right word.

black	brown	green	red
blue	gold	pink	white

1. New snow looks very _____ until it gets muddy.

2. _____ is for baby girls; blue is for baby boys.

3. Eddie didn't see that the light was _____, and the cop pulled him over.

4. The spring rains help the grass to turn _____.

5. Some people think you will have bad luck if a _____ cat crosses your path.

6. After a leaf falls from a tree, it soon turns _____.

7. On a clear day, the sky is _____.

8. When you say that you will do something, is your word as good as _____?

3 Read and Write. Put the word that does not fit with the rest on the line to the right.

1. drive   hike   run   walk   _____

2. bedroom   dream   sleep   snore   _____

3. head   hat   neck   face   _____

4. bone   hip   leg   wrist   _____

5. bake   grill   raw   roast   _____

6. bear   fox   squirrel whale   _____

7. beef   lamb   pork   shrimp   _____

8. year   fall   spring   summer   _____

9. number   pair   twice   two   _____

10. hour   minute   week   then   _____

11. jacket   shirt   pants   vest   _____

12. ditch   dune   hole   pit   _____

4 Read and Write. Put *un-* in front of the words. Write the word that is made from the two parts on the line. Then put the new word in the right sentence.

un + safe = _____   un + happy = _____

un + lucky = _____   un + wrapped = _____

1. Kate was _____ that she couldn't bake a cake that tasted any good.

2. Many people think that thirteen is an _____ number.

3. After the wreck, Kate felt _____ riding the scooter.

4. On Christmas, Billy _____ the gift from his cousin Mary first.

5 Read and Write. Put *re-* in front of the words. Write the word that is made from the two parts on the line. Then put the new word in the right sentence.

re + fuse = _____   re + main = _____

re + mind = _____   re + paid = _____

re + turn = _____

1. Kate asked Min-hee to _____ the book by Friday.

2. Eddie _____ Bob as soon as he had the money.

3. Jack could never _____ one of Aunt Louise's good dinners.

4. Billy's mother had to _____ him to make his bed each morning.

5. The teacher told Billy to _____ after class, so that she could help him with his math.

Sounds for *c* and *g*

In these words, the **c** makes a **k** sound. This is called a **hard c.**

camp	coach	curb
carry	coast	curl
cast	comb	curve

In these words, the **c** makes an **s** sound. This is called a **soft c.**

cell	city	dance
cellar	cigar	chance
center	cigarette	ounce
ceiling		bounce

In these words, the **g** is like the **g** in **gas.** This is called a **hard g.**

guess	begin	bag
guest	began	flag
guilt	begun	dog
guilty		fog

In these words, the **g** makes a **j** sound. This is called a **soft g.**

germ	range
gin	strange
ginger	stranger
gingerbread	danger

Note the sound for **dge** in these words.

badge	bridge	dodge	fudge

Words for Study

answer	groaned	happened	anybody
matter	unless	everything	anyway
question	else	hello	someday
tonight	shouldn't	anything	drinks
I'd	explain	another	coffee

Bob's Date with June

Aunt Louise stopped drying the dishes to answer the phone. When she knew it was Bob, she said, "Why, Bob, what's the matter? Your voice sounds strange."

"I feel like a dog asking you this question," said Bob, "but I wondered if you could lend me any money. I have a date tonight, and I didn't have a chance to pick up my paycheck."

"I'd love to help you out," answered Aunt Louise, "but, as a matter of fact, I'm broke, too."

"Well," groaned Bob, "I guess that's that. I can't take June to dinner unless I can get some money. Nobody else I know seems to be home."

"Don't be so silly," said Aunt Louise. "You shouldn't feel guilty just because you don't have any money. Call June up and explain what happened. I'm sure everything will be all right."

Bob was beginning to feel a little better. "You know," he said, "that's just what I'm going to do." After he had hung up, he called June at once.

"Hello," said June.

"Hi, this is Bob," said Bob. "How are you?"

"Fine," answered June. "I was just mending the top I'm going to wear tonight. Your voice sounds strange. Is anything wrong?"

"I might as well tell you," said Bob. "I don't have any money to take you out to dinner tonight. I'm really sorry." Bob was beginning to lose his nerve. He just wanted to get off the phone as fast as he could. "Maybe we can go out next week," he said as he was about to hang up.

"Wait a minute," said June. "Money's no problem. I have another idea. I like my cooking better than anybody else's anyway. In fact, I just made my first gingerbread this afternoon. I'd love for you to be the first guest to try it."

Bob was so surprised that, at first, he couldn't speak. At last he said, "Do you really want me to come over?"

"Of course," answered June. "I'll fix us a nice meal, and we can talk or see what's on television tonight. Why don't you come over around seven o'clock?"

At seven o'clock on the dot, Bob knocked on June's front door. "Hi," said June. "I'm really glad to see you. Come on in."

When Bob got home that night, he thought he had just had the best time in his whole life. He and June talked about everything—the old days, what they are doing today, and what they want to do someday. Just as Aunt Louise was always saying, "Good things can come out of bad things when people don't give up."

1 Read and Write.

ground *and* found

1. While walking in the woods, Dave _____ some money on the _____.

step *or* steep

2. "Watch your _____," said the bus driver to the people getting off the bus.

carry *or* marry

3. Bob hoped that, someday, he and June would _____.

city *and* pity

4. People who love the woods think it's a _____ that some people have to live in the _____.

steep *or* sleep

5. The hill was so _____ that the Boy Scouts decided not to climb it.

Miss, Ms., *and* Mrs.

6. A woman who is not married is called _____ or _____. A woman who is married is called _____ or _____.

carve *and* starve

7. Mary thought that if her father didn't _____ the roast beef soon, she would _____.

but *and* butter

8. Andy wanted to make himself some toast, _____ he didn't have any _____ to put on it.

sweating *and* sweater

9. Mike was _____ so badly that he decided to take off his _____.

| sprawl *or* crawl | **10.** Most babies start to _____ way before their first birthday. |

| hard *and* hardly | **11.** Mary's math homework was so _____ that she _____ had any time to watch television. |

| wood, hood, *and* stood | **12.** The farmer _____ in front of the pile of _____ with a _____ pulled over his head. |

2 Read and Write. Choose the words that have to do with meals and put them under **Meals.** Put the words that have to do with sweets under **Sweets.** Put the words that have to do with drinks under **Drinks.** *(Use each word only once.)*

candy bar	cupcake	meatballs	peppermint gum	spare ribs
coffee	French fries	milk	rice and beans	tea
Coke	ice cream cone	pear pie	roast beef	water

Meals	**Sweets**	**Drinks**
1. _____	1. _____	1. _____
2. _____	2. _____	2. _____
3. _____	3. _____	3. _____
4. _____	4. _____	4. _____
5. _____	5. _____	5. _____

3 Twelve Questions. Write *true* on the line if the sentence is true. Write *false* on the line if the sentence is false.

_____ 1. Cape Cod is on the East Coast.

_____ 2. Cats have fangs.

_____ 3. It is safe to skate on thin ice.

_____ 4. Deer can run faster than bears.

_____ 5. Food is cheaper to buy now than it was last year.

_____ 6. Popcorn is made from flour.

_____ 7. The air in a city is cleaner than the air in the woods.

_____ 8. The catcher squats behind home plate.

_____ 9. Stop signs are always red.

_____ 10. The time of day called dusk is in the morning.

_____ 11. When people blush, their faces turn blue.

_____ 12. I liked doing all the work in this reading book.

4 Read and Write. Answer these questions in good sentence form.

1. Do you put jam on your toast, or do you just use butter?

_____

2. When you don't know an answer, do you say that you don't know, or do you fake it?

_____

3. When you do your homework, do you like to write your answers, or do you like to print?

_____

4. Do you like pork chops better when they are fried or baked?

_____

5. When you get to the end of this reading book, do you plan to celebrate or take a long rest?

_____

First Review

Say these words out loud.					
slam	slap	clap	class	clay	play
drain	drop	flop	flat	flare	glare
plan	plane	plug	shrug	shrunk	skunk
cash	crash	crop	shop	shake	flake
check	cheese	chew	flew	flock	block
east	each	beach	bleach	black	quack
slice	slow	blow	blew	threw	three
drum	plum	plus	must	much	such
last	past	pest	west	waste	taste

blame	fame	flame	shame
chair	fair	hair	stair
deep	seep	sleep	steep
best	chest	west	vest
bride	pride	side	wide
dip	hip	slip	trip
brown	clown	gown	town
bunk	funk	skunk	trunk

1 Read and Write. Choose the best answer, and write it on the line.

1. Mary ate such a big lunch that she was too _____*full*_____ to eat dinner.
   a. fall   b. fell   c. fill   d. full

2. Aunt Louise asked people over to watch the big _____ on television.
   a. tame   b. same   c. name   d. game

3. Do you rest in bed when you are _____, or do you keep on working?
   a. sack   b. sick   c. soak   d. sock

4. The man was so _____ that he had to lean over to get through the door.
   a. take   b. tale   c. talk   d. tall

5. Dick went to stay with his friends on the West _____ for Christmas.
   a. Coach   b. Coal   c. Coast   d. Coat

6. "Please _____ the door, so I can save a little on my heating bill," said Jack.
   a. clock   b. close   c. cloth   d. clothes

7. Bob loved June with all his _____.
   a. hear   b. head   c. heart   d. heat

8. It seemed that no matter what Mary told Billy, her words went in one _____ and out the other.
   a. each   b. ear   c. east   d. eat

9. Danny looked all over for his laptop, but he couldn't find it _____.

   a. anybody   b. anything   c. anyway   d. anywhere

10. How many times have you _____ in town this week?

   a. beef   b. been   c. beep   d. beer   e. beet

11. Just as long as they did something that was fun, Eddie didn't

   _____ if they went to the amusement park or the movies.

   a. car   b. card   c. care   d. carry

12. Are you nice to _____ or just to your friends?

   a. ever   b. every   c. everybody   d. everything

2 Read and Write. Match the words that mean the same thing.

| cash | faint | mock | scrub | swift |
| crazy | gleam | patch | strange | useful |

_____ **1.** clean   _____ **6.** nutty

_____ **2.** fast   _____ **7.** odd

_____ **3.** handy   _____ **8.** pass out

_____ **4.** make fun of _____ **9.** shine

_____ **5.** money   _____ **10.** mend

3 Read and Write. Match the words that mean the opposite.

answer	calm	huge	tame	tired
awake	fire	loaf	thick	waste

_____ 1. full of pep

_____ 2. hire

_____ 3. question

_____ 4. save

_____ 5. small

_____ 6. sleeping

_____ 7. thin

_____ 8. upset

_____ 9. wild

_____ 10. work

4 Read and Write. Use *a* or *an* in these sentences.

1. Aunt Louise fixed herself _____ egg and two slices of toast for breakfast.

2. Billy found _____ small pile of nuts that the squirrel had stored in the tree.

3. Driving forty miles _____ hour in a school zone is unsafe.

4. Have you ever watched _____ ant carry food?

5. Mack didn't have _____ answer to Joan's question.

6. Mary's mother asked Jack to keep _____ eye on Billy while she went shopping.

7. Sue rode _____ black mule on the path in the woods.

8. Roy hoped he would get _____ leading role in the school play.

9. The Boy Scout wore his badges to _____ meeting held at the school.

10. The king wore _____ gold crown when he gave a dinner party.

5 Read and Write. Choose the words that have to do with *people* and put them under **People.** Put the words that have to do with *places* under **Places.** Put the words that have to do with *animals* under **Animals.** *(Use each word only once.)*

baby	church	deer	nurse	store
bull	coach	friend	school	whale
camp	cousin	monkey	snail	zoo

People	Places	Animals
1. _____	1. _____	1. _____
2. _____	2. _____	2. _____
3. _____	3. _____	3. _____
4. _____	4. _____	4. _____
5. _____	5. _____	5. _____

Second Review

Say these words out loud.					
brave	brain	drain	dream	cream	crime
crumb	thumb	thing	think	sink	sank
still	chill	child	mild	mind	blind
twist	wrist	wrong	strong	string	wing
much	match	catch	cost	lost	last
climb	clip	trip	train	sprain	spring
skirt	shirt	short	shout	south	sound
plate	place	plain	stain	street	such
age	cage	page	rage	wage	
class	gas	glass	grass	pass	
dare	fare	flare	spare	scare	
eel	feel	keel	peel	wheel	
file	mile	pile	smile	while	
cry	dry	fly	fry	why	
clip	dip	hip	zip	whip	
blow	flow	low	slow	show	

1 Read and Write. Choose the best answer, and write it on the line.

1. Roy was a brave man, but when he saw a mouse, he felt _____.
   a. harmless   b. helpless   c. hopeless   d. careless

2. Kate is very _____ when she rides her new scooter.
   a. careful   b. harmful   c. helpful   d. useful

3. After he fell off his bike, the boy ran _____ to find his mother.
   a. firmly   b. quickly   c. lovely   d. friendly   e. safely

4. The fuse box was in the _____ near the two old tubs.
   a. cellar   b. center   c. splinter   d. stranger

5. "_____ the last time I try to bake a cake," said Kate firmly.
   a. Don't   b. Won't   c. That's   d. What's

6. "_____ only got twenty minutes to eat lunch today," said Dan.
   a. I   b.   I'll c.   I'm   d. I've

7. "_____ I see you downtown yesterday?" asked Min-hee.
   a. Can't   b. Didn't   c. Couldn't   d. Shouldn't

8. "If you want to be a _____, you must know a lot about words,"
   said Mary's father.
   a. winner   b. wonder   c. worker   d. writer

9. When the fighter's eye started to bleed, they knew it would be
   _____ if he went on fighting.
   a. unhappy   b. unlucky   c. unsafe   d. unwrap

10. Aunt Louise said that feeling _____ about hurting a friend's
    feelings is a waste of time. Just say you're sorry and get on with your life.
    a. guilty   b. lucky   c. needy   d. rosy

2 Numbers. Use this list of words to answer the questions. (You will not need to use all the words on the list.)

one	six	eleven	sixteen	thirty
two	seven	twelve	seventeen	forty
three	eight	thirteen	eighteen	sixty
four	nine	fourteen	nineteen	ninety
five	ten	fifteen	twenty	millions

_____ **1.** How many months are in a year?

_____ **2.** How many days are in a week?

_____ **3.** How many minutes are in an hour?

_____ **4.** How many hours do you meet each week with your teacher?

_____ **5.** What do some people think is an unlucky number?

_____ **6.** What do you think is a lucky number?

_____ **7.** What is the sum of thirteen plus three?

_____ **8.** How many lungs do you have?

_____ **9.** How many spleens do you have?

_____ **10.** How many stars are there in the sky?

3 Read and Write. Choose the right answers, and write them on the lines.

1. Mother is to woman as _____*father*_____ is to man.
   a. brother   b. father   c. female   d. male

2. Shirt is to arms as pants are to _____.
   a. clothes   b. legs   c. men   d. feet

3. Beef is to cow as pork is to _____.
   a. chops   b. ham   c. lamb   d. pig

4. Yell is to scream as stay is to _____.
   a. remain   b. remind   c. refuse   d. relax

5. Most is to least as best is to _____.
   a. bad   b. badly   c. worse   d. worst

6. Calm is to relaxed as mad is to _____.
   a. cope   b. mistake   c. tired   d. upset

7. Ground is to sky as floor is to _____.
   a. ceiling   b. house   c. room   d. top

8. Deer is to swift as _____ is to slow.
   a. monkey   b. skunk   c. snail   d. squirrel

4 Word Pairs. Use a word from **A** to put on the first line. Use a word from **B** to put on the last line.

A
bat
black
bride
cake
cats
gas
knife
reading
salt
Saturday
soap
thick

B
ball
blue
dogs
fork
groom
ice cream
oil
pepper
Sunday
thin
water
writing

1. Many people put these on their food.

   _____salt_____ and _____pepper_____

2. You watch them get married.

   _____ and _____

3. This is the weekend.

   _____ and _____

4. You use these when you eat dinner.

   _____ and _____

5. To play baseball, you need these.

   _____ and _____

6. You can clean many things with this.

   _____ and _____

7. What are you learning more about in this class?

   _____ and _____

8. Most cars need these two things to run.

   _____ and _____

9. If you're hurt badly, your skin turns

   _____ and _____ .

10. Some people fight like _____ and
    _____ .

11. Some people eat this at a birthday party.

    _____ and _____

12. Good friends see you through

    _____ and _____ .

5 Read and Write. Answer these questions in good sentence form.

1. Are you most happy in a big city, a small town, or the woods?

_____

2. Do you use cream in your coffee, or do you think black coffee tastes better?

_____

3. Do you think men are better drivers than women, or do you think women are better drivers?

_____

4. When you feel you are in danger, do you freeze, or do you run for your life?

_____

5. Which do you like best at an amusement park: the games, the rides, or the food?

_____

6. Are you careful with money, or do you spend it as fast as you get it?

_____

7. Do you think there should be a law to stop people from using cell phones while they drive, or do you think people should make up their own minds?

_____

8. What do you think of the work you have done in this reading book?

_____

9. Do you like telling other people how you feel about things, or do you like keeping your thoughts to yourself?

_____

Word Index: Lessons 1–20

A

a
able
about
according
ace
across
act
ad
add
address
after
afternoon
again
age
ago
aid
ail
air
all
all right
almost
alone
also
always
am
amuse
amusement
an
and
Andy
animal
another
answer
ant
any
anybody
anything
anyway
anywhere
are
aren't
arm
around
art
as
ask
at
ate
auction
aunt
awake
away
awoke

B

baby
back
bad
badge
badly
bag
bake
Baker
bald
ball
band
bang
bank
banker
bar
bare
bark
barn
base
baseball
bat
batch
bath
bathroom
be
beach
bean
bear
beat
because
Becky
bed
bedroom
beef
been
beep
beer
beet
before
began
begin
begun
behind
bell
belt
Ben
bent
best
bet
better
bib
bid
big
bike

bill
Billy
bind
birth
birthday
bit
bite
black
blame
bleach
bleed
bless
blew
blind
block
blow
blue
blush
board
boarder
boat
Bob
boil
bolt
bomb
bond
bone
bony
book
bore
born
both
bounce
bow
box
boy
boyfriend
brain
brakes
brave
bread
breakfast
breath
breathless
bride
bridge
broke
brother
brown
buck
bud
bug
bulb
bull
bum
bump

bumper
bumpy
bun
bunk
bunt
burn
burst
bus
bus stop
but
butter
buy
by

C

cab
cage
cake
call
calm
calmly
came
camp
can
candy
cane
can't
cap
cape
Cape Cod
car
card
care
careful
careless
carry
cart
carve
case
cash
casino
cast
cat
catch
catcher
ceiling
celebrate
cell
cell phone
cellar
cent
center
chair
chance
charm
chart

Chase
chase
cheap
check
checkbook
cheese
chest
chew
child
chill
choose
chop
Christmas
chrome
chronic
church
cigar
cigarette
city
clap
class
classroom
clay
clean
cleaner
clear
climb
clip
clock
close
cloth
clothes
clown
club
coach
coal
coast
coat
cod
code
coffee
Coke
cold
comb
come
computer
cone
cook
cookbook
cool
cop
cope
copper
corn
cost
cot

could
couldn't
count
course
court
cousin
cow
crash
crawl
crazy
cream
crib
crime
crop
cross
crown
crumb
cry
cub
cube
cup
cupcake
curb
curl
curtain
curve
cut
cute

D

dab
dad
dam
damp
Dan
dance
danger
Danny
dare
dark
date
Dave
day
daylight
dead
deal
dear
death
decide
deck
deep
deer
den
dent
desk
dice

Dick
did
didn't
die
dig
dime
dine
diner
dining room
dinner
dip
dirt
dirty
dish
ditch
dive
do
dock
dodge
does
dog
done
donkey
don't
door
doorway
dope
dot
down
downstairs
downtown
doze
Dr.
drain
dream
dress
drink
drive
driver
drop
drove
drum
dry
duck
due
dues
dug
duke
dull
dumb
dump
dune
dunk
during
dusk
Dutch

E

each
ear
east
easy
eat
Eddie
eel
egg
eight
eighteen
eleven
else
Elvis
end
enough
even
evening
ever
everybody
everything
explain
eye

F

face
fact
fad
fade
fail
faint
fair
fake
fall
false
fame
fan
fang
far
fare
farm
farmer
fast
fat
father
fed
fee
feed
feel
feet
fell
felt
female
fetch
few
fib
fifteen

fifty
fig
fight
fighter
file
fill
find
fine
fire
firm
firmly
first
fish
fist
fit
five
fix
flag
flake
flame
flare
flat
flew
flip
flock
floor
flop
flour
flow
flush
fly
fog
fond
food
fool
foot
for
forget
fork
fortune
fortune-teller
forty
found
four
fourteen
fox
free
freeze
French
French fries
fresh
Friday
friend
friendly
from
front
froze
fry

fudge
full
fume
fun
fund(s)
funk
funny
fuse
fuss
fussy

G

game
gas
gate
gave
germ
get
gift
gin
ginger
gingerbread
girl
girlfriend
give
glad
gland
glare
glass
gleam
glue
go
goal
gold
gong
good
goodness
got
gotten
gown
grade
grape
grass
gray
green
grill
groan
groom
ground
guess
guest
guilt
guilty
gum
gun
guy

H

had
hadn't
hair
haircut
hall
ham
hammer
hand
handle
handy
hang
happen
happy
hard
hardly
harm
harmful
harmless
has
hat
hate
have
haven't
hay
he
head
hear
heart
heat
heck
heel
held
hello
helmet
help
helper
helpful
helpless
hen
her
herd
here
herself
hi
hid
hide
high
high school
hike
hill
him
himself
hint
hip
hire
his

hit
hock
hole
home
homework
honk
hood
hop
hope
hopeless
horn
hose
hot
hour
house
how
however
hug
huge
hum
hung
hunt
hunter
hurt
hut

I

I
ice
ice cream
icy
I'd
idea
if
ill
I'll
I'm
in
ink
inside
Internet
into
is
it
itch
it's
I've

J

jab
Jack
jacket
jail
jam
jar
jaw
jazz
jeans

jeep
jeer
jerk
Joan
job
jobless
join
joint
joke
joker
Jones
jot
joy
jug
jump
June
junk
just

K

Kate
keel
keep
keeper
ketchup
key
kick
kid
kind
king
kiss
kit
kite
knee
kneecap
knew
knife
knock
knot
know
known

L

lab
lace
lack
laid
lake
lamb
lame
lamp
land
lane
lap
laptop
lark
last
late

later
laugh
law
lay
lead
leaf
leak
lean
learn
least
leave
led
left
leg
lend
lent
less
let
let's
lick
lid
lie
life
lift
light
like
lime
limp
line
lint
lip
list
lit
little
live
load
loaf
lobby
lock
lone
long
look
lose
lost
lot(s)
loud
loudly
Louise
love
loveliest
lovely
low
loyal
luck
lucky
lug
lump
lunch

lung

M

Mack
mad
made
maid
mail
main
make
male
mall
man
many
Mark
mark
marry
Mary
mask
mat
match
mate
math
matter
may
maybe
me
meal
mean
meat
meatball
meet
meeting
melt
men
mend
mess
messy
met
mice
middle
might
Mike
mile
mild
milk
million
mind
mine
Min-hee
mint
minute
miss
mistake
mitt
mix

mob
mock
mole
mom
Monday
money
monkey
month
mood
moon
mop
more
morning
most
mother
mouse
movie
Mr.
Mrs.
Ms.
much
mud
muddy
mug
muggy
mule
muse
must
mute
my
myself

N

nail
name
nap
near
neat
neck
need
needy
nerve
net
never
new
next
nice
nick
nickname
night
nine
nineteen
ninety
no
nobody
nod

none
noon
nope
north
nose
nosy
not
note
notebook
nothing
now
nude
numb
number
nurse
nut
nutty

O

oar
o'clock
odd
of
off
often
oh
oil
okay
old
on
once
one
online
only
open
opposite
or
other
ounce
our
out
outside
oven
over
own
owner

P

pace
pack
pad
page
paid
pain
paint
painter

pair
pale
palm
pan
pancake
pant
pants
park
parking lot
part
party
pass
past
pat
patch
path
paw
pay
paycheck
payday
payment
pea
pear
peck
peek
peel
peer
pen
people
pep
pepper
peppermint
pest
pet
phone
pick
picture
pie
piece
pig
pile
pill
pin
pine
pink
pit
pity
place
plain
plan
plane
plate
play
please
plug
plum
plus

pod
poke
pole
pond
pool
poor
pop
popcorn
pork
pork chop
pot
pour
pray
price
pride
print
prize
problem
proud
prune
pull
pulse
pump
punt
purse
put

Q

quack
question
quick
quickly
quit
quite

R

race
rack
rage
raid
rain
raincoat
rake
ram
ramp
ran
rang
range
rank
rare
rat
rate
raw
reach
read
ready

real
really
red
reel
refund
refuse
relax
remain
remind
rent
repay
rest
restroom
return
rib
rice
rich
rid
ride
rig
right
ring
rip
ripe
risk
road
roar
roast
roast beef
rob
robe
rock
rod
rode
role
roll
room
rope
rose
rosy
rot
row
Roy
royal
rub
rude
rug
rule
ruler
run
rung
runt
rush

S

sack

sad
safe
safely
said
sale
salt
same
sand
Sandy
sandy
sang
sank
sat
Saturday
save
saw
say
scar
scare
scared
school
school bus
scooter
score
scout
scramble
scratch
scream
screech
screen
scrub
search
seat
second
see
seed
seek
seem
seen
seep
self
sell
send
sent
serve
set
seven
seventeen
shake
shame
shape
she
shift
shine
shiny
shirt
shock

shook
shop
short
should
shouldn't
shout
show
shred
shrimp
shrank
shrink
shrug
shrunk
shut
sick
side
sigh
sight
silly
since
sing
singer
sink
sip
sit
six
sixteen
sixty
skate
skill
skin
skirt
skunk
sky
slam
slap
sleep
sleeve
slice
slip
slow
slush
small
smart
smash
smell
smile
smoke
snail
snake
sneeze
snore
snow
so
soak
soap
sob

sock
soft
some
someday
something
song
soon
sore
sorry
sort
sound
sour
south
space
spank
spare
spare ribs
speak
speed
spend
spent
spill
spite
splash
spleen
splint
splinter
split
spoon
spot
spotless
sprain
sprang
sprawl
spring
sprint
squat
squash
squeal
squeeze
squirrel
stage
stain
stair
star
stare
start
starve
stay
steak
steep
step
still
stomach
stood
stop

store
storm
story
straight
strain
strange
stranger
strap
straw
stream
street
streetlight
strict
strike
string
stroke
strong
struggle
stuff
sub
such
suddenly
suds
Sue
sum
summer
sun
sunburn
Sunday
sung
sunk
sunny
sure
surf
surfer
surprise
swear
sweat
sweater
sweet
swerve
swift
swim
switch

T

tab
tack
tail
take
tale
talk
tall
tame
tan
tank

tap
tar
task
taste
tax
tea
teacher
tear
teeth
television
tell
teller
temper
ten
tent
test
than
thank
thankful
that
that's
the
their
them
then
there
these
they
thick
thin
thing
think
thinker
third
thirteen
thirty
this
those
thought
three
threw
through
throw
thumb
Thursday
tick
ticket
tide
tie
tight
tile
Tim
time
timeless
tin
tire
to

toast
toaster
today
told
Tom
tone
tonight
too
took
tool
tooth
top
tore
torn
toward
town
toy
trail
train
tray
treat
tree
trip
truck
true
trunk
trust
try
tub
tube
Tuesday
tug
tune
turn
twelve
twenty
twice
twin
twist
two

U

unhappy
unless
unlucky
unsafe
until
unwrap
up
upset
us
use
useful

V

van

verse
very
vest
voice
vote
voter

W

wade
wage
wait
wake
walk
want
was
wasn't
waste
watch
watchful
water
wave
way
we
wear
web
wed
Wednesday
weed
week
weekend
weekly
weep
well
went
were
west
wet
whale
what
what's
wheat
wheel
when
where
which
while
whip
white
who
whole
why
wide
wife
wig
wild
will

win
wind
wine
wing
wink
winner
wipe
wire
wiry
wish
witch
with
without
woke
woman
women
won
wonder
won't
wood
word
wore
work
worker
worn
worry
worse
worst
would
wow
wrap
wreck
wrist
write
writer
wrong
wrote

X

Y

year
yell
yes
yesterday
yet
you
your
you're
yourself

Z

zip
zone
zoo

Answer Key

Lesson 1

1 Copying Sentences
See student text.

2 Word Sounds
1. Tim, time
2. tube, tub
3. not, note
4. Can, cane
5. quit, quite

Lesson 2

1 Copying Sentences
See student text.

2 Word Sounds
1. huge
2. cut
3. met
4. us
5. cope
6. rode
7. hopes
8. at

Lesson 3

1 Marking the Vowels
1. fir̸e
2. sĭp
3. cān̸e
4. nīc̸e
5. wōk̸e
6. sŭn
7. hōl̸e
8. bĕd
9. āt̸e
10. ūs̸e
11. mē
12. lĭd
13. jăb
14. cūt̸e
15. kēep
16. rūl̸e

2 Word Sounds
1. mad, mud, made
2. hot, hates, hat
3. six, sit, sip
4. cop, cope, cup
5. man, men, mine
6. us, fuse, used
7. at, as, am
8. late, dates, Kate
9. pet, pep, pen

Lesson 4

1 Word Sounds
1. cute
2. tub
3. rod
4. Cape
5. ripe
6. rid
7. wine
8. fad
9. hope
10. fuss
11. let
12. feel
13. hot
14. ham
15. feed

2 Yes or No
Answers will vary.

Lesson 5

1 Adding -ed
1. looked
2. lasted
3. talked
4. asked
5. messed
6. relaxed

1. faced
2. saved
3. joked
4. hired
5. lined
6. refused

1. hopped
2. sipped
3. patted
4. gunned
5. popped
6. sobbed

2 Word Sounds
1. phone
2. bus
3. sale
4. bed
5. pan
6. red
7. cane
8. hut
9. bone
10. hugs
11. horn
12. name
13. park
14. lap

Lesson 6

1 Adding -ed
1. called
2. hunted
3. landed
4. walked
5. dumped
6. ended

1. baked
2. named
3. liked
4. dated
5. tired
6. hoped

1. rubbed
2. kidded
3. ripped
4. netted
5. topped
6. rammed

2 Word Sounds
1. sick
2. spent
3. find
4. bucks
5. lamp
6. fond
7. luck
8. hand
9. picked
10. mind
11. end

Lesson 7

1 Adding -ing
1. going
2. fixing
3. singing
4. looking
5. missing

1. taking
2. having
3. living
4. joking
5. hoping

1. running
2. sipping
3. patting
4. jabbing
5. hopping

2 Word Sounds
1. fat, cat, sat
2. big, pig
3. mole, hole
4. ran, ran, fan
5. Kate, late, date
6. gave, wave
7. thank, bank
8. kind, remind, wind
9. lamp, camp
10. pale, sale
11. man, ran, van
12. find, fond

Lesson 8

1 Word Sounds
1. code
2. fox
3. dam
4. pad
5. dive
6. tame
7. rate
8. dined

2 Using a and an
1. an
2. a
3. a
4. an
5. an
6. a
7. a
8. a
9. an
10. an

3 Marking the Vowels

1. fūmé
2. lĕss
3. nĕck
4. rōbé
5. tĭck
6. hănd
7. sŏck
8. sāfé
9. quĭck
10. cĕnt
11. mīnd
12. rēfūsé
13. ŭs
14. bēef
15. fēmālé

4 Words That Mean the Same

1. huge
2. keep
3. seek
4. honk
5. six
6. jab
7. fix
8. fun
9. weep
10. females

5 Writing Sentences

Answers will vary.

Lesson 9

1 Adding -y to Words

1. messy
2. fussy
3. bumpy
4. needy
5. sandy

1. icy
2. nosy
3. dirty
4. bony
5. wiry

1. funny
2. sunny
3. Danny
4. muggy
5. nutty

2 Words That End in -ly

1. quickly
2. lovely
3. safely
4. friendly
5. weekly

3 Words That End in -y

1. baby
2. candy
3. sixty
4. lobby
5. ninety
6. Andy
7. muddy
8. handy
9. forty
10. Becky

4 Words That Mean the Same

1. hide
2. behind
3. ten cents
4. male
5. not happy
6. mock
7. joke
8. refuse
9. funny
10. funds
11. Sunday
12. Saturday

Lesson 10

1 Word Sounds

1. gas, pass
2. thumb, numb
3. None, one, done
4. knew, few, new
5. right, lights, night
6. see, fee, knee
7. wrote, note, vote
8. heck, neck, wreck
9. dock, locked, knock
10. lay, way, day

2 Word Opposites

1. night
2. last
3. back
4. bad
5. sad
6. huge
7. wrong
8. play
9. there
10. same

3 Word Study

1. yesterday
2. friend
3. foot
4. ant
5. sun
6. females
7. wine
8. numb
9. cot
10. fit

Lesson 11

1 Adding -er to Words

1. quicker
2. tighter
3. teller
4. boxer
5. hunter
6. herder

1. finer
2. ruder
3. cuter
4. baker
5. later
6. diner

1. bigger
2. fatter
3. hotter
4. winner
5. hitter
6. mugger

2 Words That End in -er

1. bumper
2. hammer
3. Copper
4. summer
5. pepper
6. ruler
7. worker
8. better, better

3 Changing y to i and Adding -er

handier
happier
luckier

lovelier
fussier
bumpier

1. luckier
2. happier
3. lovelier
4. fussier
5. bumpier
6. handier

4 Who Does What?

1. a hunter
2. a writer
3. a surfer
4. a singer
5. a joker
6. a banker
7. a fighter
8. a catcher
9. a thinker

Lesson 12

1 Context Clues

five, work, house
eat, meat, boiled, tea, mug, fork
soap, water, night

2 Word Sounds

1. deer
2. road
3. due
4. far
5. barn
6. ails
7. load
8. peas
9. soak
10. moon
11. pain
12. foot
13. maid
14. real
15. mouse
16. coals
17. main
18. cared
19. bored
20. hard

3 Writing Sentences

Answers will vary.

Lesson 13

1 Word Sounds

1. moon
2. noon
3. soon
4. mail
5. main
6. maid
7. carve
8. cart
9. card
10. meat
11. meal
12. mean
13. code
14. cope
15. cone
16. tore
17. sore
18. wore
19. more
20. leak
21. lean
22. lead
23. leaf
24. worn
25. horn
26. corn
27. torn
28. born

2 Words That End in -er

1. painter
2. keeper
3. catcher
4. boarder
5. voter
6. diner
7. helper
8. teacher
9. teller

3 Word Study

1. head
2. year
3. pear
4. dice
5. oven
6. air
7. food
8. tea
9. fake
10. wages
11. dark
12. bumper

4 Marking the Vowels

1. ădd
2. bīte̸
3. gāte̸
4. dămp
5. sĕnd
6. clŏck
7. pŏp
8. sāme̸
9. fūme̸
10. rēel
11. hīke̸
12. hŭnt
13. dōze̸
14. dŭnk
15. zōne̸
16. dĕck

Lesson 14

1 The Ending -ful

harmful   careful
helpful   useful
watchful   thankful

1. helpful
2. watchful
3. harmful
4. useful
5. thankful
6. careful

2 The Ending -less

harmless   breathless
helpless   careless
hopeless   timeless

1. timeless
2. breathless
3. careless
4. hopeless
5. helpless
6. harmless

3 Words That Mean the Same

1. carve
2. ill
3. handy
4. street
5. soaked
6. shout
7. hurt
8. bare
9. poor
10. dead

4 Word Opposites

1. cold
2. start
3. inside
4. worse
5. take
6. messy
7. never
8. false
9. dumb
10. harmless

5 Compound Words

1. lab coat
2. all right
3. candy canes
4. soap suds
5. bunk beds
6. bear cub
7. cell phone
8. car keys
9. parking lot
10. birthday cake
11. dining room
12. school bus
13. art class

Lesson 15

1 The Ending -est

1. nearest
2. cheapest
3. richest
4. smartest
5. shortest
1. finest
2. safest
3. rudest
4. ripest
5. latest
1. biggest
2. hottest
3. fattest
4. maddest
5. saddest

2 Changing y to i and Adding -est

funniest   luckiest
happiest   dirtiest
easiest

1. easiest
2. dirtiest
3. luckiest
4. happiest
5. funniest

3 Words That Mean the Same

1. wish
2. easy
3. torn
4. tug
5. piece
6. auction
7. chair
8. slam
9. people
10. must

4 Word Sounds

1. stuff
2. odd
3. stare
4. cash
5. dumb
6. fast
7. much
8. cheap
9. desk
10. sell
11. wish
12. search

Lesson 16

1 Word Sounds

1. slip, hip
2. flip, rip
3. pale
4. male, sale
5. stale, tales
6. bump, dump
7. pump
8. jump, lump
9. rage
10. wage, age
11. stage
12. page
13. plain, pain
14. rain, Main
15. stains
16. shame, lame
17. came, name
18. blamed, same
19. glare, scared
20. care, rare
21. stare
22. rush
23. slush
24. blushed
25. hair, stairs
26. chair
27. fair, air

2 Compound Words

1. paycheck
2. peppermint
3. daylight
4. restroom
5. kneecap
6. raincoat
7. checkbook
8. pancakes
9. haircut
10. nickname

3 Writing Sentences

Answers will vary.

Lesson 17

1 Word Sounds

1. blow
2. flow
3. slow, row
4. price
5. pride, prizes
6. toast
7. taste, tested
8. best
9. chest, vests
10. pests
11. clown, gown, brown
12. trunk
13. truck
14. trust
15. harming
16. farm, charming
17. clay, may
18. prayed, hay
19. drops, stopped
20. crops
21. gum, plum
22. drum

2 Putting Words in Classes

Town	School	Farm
bus stops	classes	barn
churches	desks	cows
parks	homework	crops
stores	reading	hay
street lights	teachers	pigs

3 Best and Least

Answers will vary.

Lesson 18

1 Word Sounds

1. lift
2. left
3. gift
4. shift
5. math, bath
6. path
7. hill
8. spilled
9. grilled
10. chill
11. dare
12. fare
13. spare
14. flares
15. know, blow
16. throw
17. snow
18. fibs
19. bib, crib
20. ribs
21. toast
22. coast
23. roast

2 Numbers

1. eighteen
2. twenty
3. fifteen
4. fifteen
5. sixteen
6. eleven
7. fifteen
8. seven
9. four
10. thirteen
11. seven
12. twelve
13. Answers may vary.
14. four (or five counting the spare)
15. Answers will vary.
16. Answers will vary.
17. Answers will vary.
18. Answers will vary.
19. Answers will vary.
20. nine

3 Compound Words

1. weekend
2. sunburn
3. bathroom
4. notebook
5. popcorn
6. bedroom
7. baseball
8. cookbook
9. classroom
10. downstairs

Lesson 19

1 Word Sounds

1. wrist
2. splint
3. scared
4. helmet
5. scratches
6. squash
7. spotless
8. squirrels
9. brakes
10. chronic
11. seen
12. test

2 Colors

1. white
2. Pink
3. red
4. green
5. black
6. brown
7. blue
8. gold

3 Which Word Does Not Fit?

1. drive
2. bedroom
3. hat
4. bone
5. raw
6. whale
7. shrimp
8. year
9. number
10. then
11. pants
12. dune

4 Words That Begin with *un-*

unsafe   unhappy
unlucky   unwrapped

1. unhappy
2. unlucky
3. unsafe
4. unwrapped

5 Words That Begin with *re-*

refuse   remain
remind   repaid
return

1. return
2. repaid
3. refuse
4. remind
5. remain

Lesson 20

1 Word Sounds

1. found, ground
2. step
3. marry
4. pity, city
5. steep
6. Ms., Miss, Ms., Mrs.
7. carve, starve
8. but, butter
9. sweating, sweater
10. crawl
11. hard, hardly
12. stood, wood, hood

2 Putting Words in Classes

Meals	Sweets	Drinks
French fries	candy bar	coffee
meatballs	cupcake	Coke
rice and beans	ice cream cone	milk
roast beef	pear pie	tea
spare ribs	peppermint gum	water

3 Twelve Questions

1. true
2. true
3. false
4. Either true or false
5. false
6. false
7. false
8. true
9. true
10. false
11. false
12. Answers will vary.

4 Writing Sentences

Answers will vary.

First Review

1 Choosing the Best Answer

1. full
2. game
3. sick
4. tall
5. Coast
6. close
7. heart
8. ear
9. anywhere
10. been
11. care
12. everybody

2 Words That Mean the Same

1. scrub
2. swift
3. useful
4. mock
5. cash
6. crazy
7. strange
8. faint
9. gleam
10. patch

3 Word Opposites

1. tired
2. fire
3. answer
4. waste
5. huge
6. awake
7. thick
8. calm
9. tame
10. loaf

4 Using *a* and *an*

1. an
2. a
3. an
4. an
5. an
6. an
7. a
8. a
9. a
10. a

5 Putting Words in Classes

People	Places	Animals
baby	camp	bull
coach	church	deer
cousin	school	monkey
friend	store	snail
nurse	zoo	whale

Second Review

1 Choosing the Best Answer

1. helpless
2. careful
3. quickly
4. cellar
5. That's
6. I've
7. Didn't
8. writer
9. unsafe
10. guilty

2 Numbers

1. twelve
2. seven
3. sixty
4. Answers will vary.
5. thirteen
6. Answers will vary.
7. sixteen
8. two
9. one
10. millions

3 Which Word Fits Best?

1. father
2. legs
3. pig
4. remain
5. worst
6. upset
7. ceiling
8. snail

4 Word Pairs

1. salt and pepper
2. bride and groom
3. Saturday and Sunday
4. knife and fork
5. bat and ball
6. soap and water
7. reading and writing
8. gas and oil
9. black and blue
10. cats and dogs
11. cake and ice cream
12. thick and thin

5 Writing Sentences

Answers will vary.